IR

D0340860

# BETTER LIVING
# THROUGH
# SCIENCE

## THE BASIC SCIENTIFIC PRINCIPLES
## YOU NEED TO SOLVE
## EVERY HOUSEHOLD CONUNDRUM

## MARK FRARY

RODALE

© 2010 by Elwin Street Limited

Conceived and produced by
Elwin Street Limited
144 Liverpool Road
London N1 1LA
www.elwinstreet.com

Rodale books may be purchased for business or promotional use or for special sales. For information, please write to:
Special Markets Department, Rodale Inc., 733 Third Avenue, New York, NY 10017

Printed in the United States of America
Rodale Inc. makes every effort to use acid-free ⊗, recycled paper ♻.

**Library of Congress Cataloging-in-Publication Data**
Frary, Mark.
  Better living through science : the basic scientific principles you
need to solve every household conundrum / Mark Frary.
      p. cm.
  Includes index.
  ISBN-13: 978–1–60529–192–5 hardcover
  ISBN-10: 1–60529–192–7 hardcover
  1.  Science—Miscellanea.  I. Title.
  Q173.F82 2010
  500—dc22

                                        2010024090


Printed in China

We inspire and enable people to improve their lives and the world around them.

# BETTER LIVING THROUGH SCIENCE

# Contents

# Prepare to be enlightened...

Did you ever daydream at school, stuck in a math or science class, feeling confused or bored, and certain that you'd never need to understand such things in the real world? Chances are, like most of us, that's how you felt then, and maybe even now.

Well, prepare to be astounded. The things you learned (or didn't learn) in those classes might now seem even more irrelevant to your everyday life, but that couldn't be more wrong. If you've ever wanted to know how to cut back on household bills, struggled to keep your possessions or paperwork under control, or wished you could make better use of the chaos that is your garden, then you've come to the right place. Science is your secret weapon!

This book will take you through some scientific principles, step by simple step, and show you how easy it is to apply them to improve the quality of your life.

Your kitchen cupboard is probably full of fluids containing all sorts of weird, wonderful, and expensive chemicals. Chemistry can tell you how they work and whether you actually need any of them, and when a simple household staple will do the job just as well for a fraction of the cost, leaving you with far less clutter.

Use geometry to find out whether furniture will fit around tight corners at

> "Things should be made as simple as possible, but not any simpler."
> EINSTEIN

home, or what's the best way to wrap presents—even those awkwardly shaped ones—and how to make wrapping stretch to cover that last Christmas gift.

Physics comes to the rescue in the kitchen. Want to know why your soufflés and cakes don't rise? Science has the answers and can help you become the envy of your dinner party guests. Years of experience in the kitchen will get you so far but science can help you cheat.

Math comes in very handy when working out the best way to pay off your credit card debt, or understanding what makes a ball spin to better your chances of hitting a home run.

Don't worry if the very thought of an equation fills you with fear. You don't need to be adept at algebra or a connoisseur of calculus. This book explains things in an easy-to-understand manner that can be enjoyed by anyone, no matter what grades you got back in school.

# How to get a sofa around a corner

It has happened to us all…well at least all of us who are not mathematicians. I'm talking about what is generally known to mathematicians as a spatial awareness problem and to the rest of us as the sofa problem—also known as the "I could have sworn it would fit" scenario.

Picture this. You are out shopping at your local furniture store and there's a sale on. You see a sofa that you really like, and, amazingly, it's on sale at 80 percent off. You just have to buy it.

The next day when it is delivered, you realize there could be a problem. The sofa gets through the door to your apartment, but there is an L-shaped corridor between the door and the living room, and the sofa, despite hours of pushing and pulling, just won't fit. You return to the store the following day, only to find out that there are no refunds on sale items. Your aunt upstate is very grateful to receive it the following week at her old house with beautifully straight, broad corridors while your bank manager is less than impressed when you have to buy another one that does fit.

## Simplify the problem

So why don't mathematicians have the same problem? It's all a matter of geometry—the mathematics of lines, curves, and shapes. If you thought geometry was just for schoolkids and academics in ivory towers, think again. Knowing geometry can save your back and your bank balance. A bit of algebra will come in handy here too—all you need to remember is that you can represent variable lengths by letter symbols.

Often, mathematicians try to understand more difficult problems by considering easier ones. Rather than trying to fit a

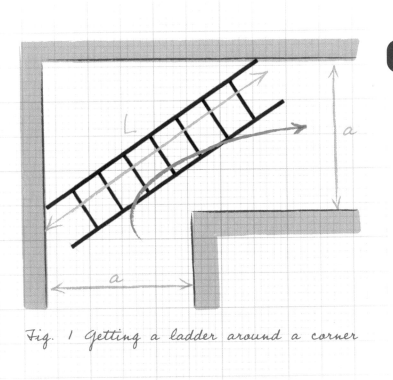

*Fig. 1 Getting a ladder around a corner*

sofa around a corner, let's try getting a ladder of length $L$ around the corner, held on its side. Let's also imagine that the two corridors are both the same width, which we will denote by the letter $a$.

Symmetrical considerations should make it obvious that the critical point is where the ladder just scrapes the inner corner and has an equal length on both sides (see Fig. 1). This means that the length from the outer corner to the ends of the ladder is $2a$.

The Pythagorean theorem—which we should remember from school—tells us that:

$$L^2 = (2a)^2 + (2a)^2$$

or $L = \sqrt{8}a$, something that can be easily worked out on a calculator.

For corridors of unequal size, we must refer to a math paper called "Moving a Rectangle around a Corner—Geometrically" by Raymond Boute of the University of Ghent, in Belgium.

If we say the width of one corridor is $a$ and the width of the other corridor is $b$ (see diagram on the opposite page), then with a bit of mathematical wizardry we can work out what the length ($L$) of the longest ladder is that can fit round the corner.

Boute shows that by considering the rotation of the ladder around the corner, the length of the longest ladder is then given by the equation:

$$L^2 = (a^{2/3} + b^{2/3})^3$$

or

$$L = (a^{2/3} + b^{2/3})^{3/2}$$

A scientific calculator can help you work this out.

## From ladders to sofas

Moving from a ladder to a sofa of width $w$ (see Fig. 2) makes the mathematics horribly complicated. Boute says you need to work out the values for $m$ that satisfy the following equation.

$$(bm^3 - a)^2 - w^2 (m^2 - 1)^2 (m^2 + 1) = 0$$

Once you have worked out the value of $m$, then the maximum length of the sofa is given by:

$$L^2 = (1 + 1/m^2) (a + mb - w(m^2 + 1))$$

So there's the math if you feel like a challenge. Thankfully, however, you don't have to go through all of the math yourself. The Internet can provide you with a quicker way: To download a calculator to do the math for you, visit http://demonstrations

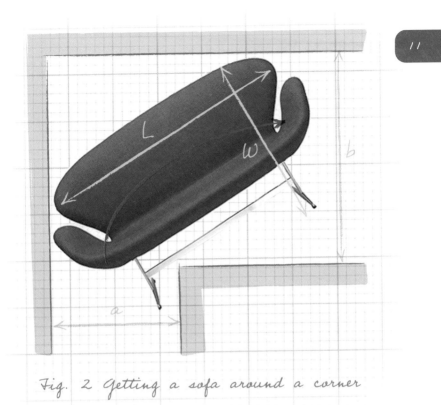

*Fig. 2 Getting a sofa around a corner*

.wolfram.com/MovingACouchAroundACorner/. Simply enter the values for your corridor widths and the length and width of your sofa and you can see whether it will fit.

Mathematicians like challenges and they have now moved on from boring old rectangular sofas to work out what the biggest (in terms of area) sofa is you can get around the corner. A mathematician named J. Gerver has come up with the biggest so far. It looks like an old-fashioned telephone, with a semi-circular front and a curved back.

So next time you go to the furniture store, don't forget to take some measurements. Or bring along a friendly mathematician.

# How to combat garlic breath

It is a problem as old as time. Ever since humans started to eat garlic, or *Allium sativum* to give its botanical name, those close to them have had to deal with the resultant garlic breath.

## The science behind the smell

Over the years, garlic has earned the unfortunate name of the stinking rose, and it's no surprise. Garlic's distinctive smell is caused by a compound called allicin, chemically known as 2-propene-1-sulfinothioic acid S-2-propenyl ester.

Perhaps surprisingly, allicin does not occur naturally in garlic— it is only created when you crush or cut a bulb. These actions break open compartments in the garlic that contain two chemicals called alliinase and alliin that are normally kept isolated from one another. This is why a garlic bulb does not have that distinctive smell. It is also why foods cooked with whole garlic bulbs are often less aromatic than those using crushed garlic.

The mechanism for garlic breath is detailed in a 1999 study by Dr. Fabrizis Suarez and colleagues at the University of Minnesota. When you eat garlic, allicin reaches the stomach and is broken down into a number of different compounds. Most of these are then broken down further by the intestine and liver and are passed out of the body.

However, this process also creates a noxious gas called allyl methyl sulfide, or AMS, which does not get broken down in the same way. Instead, AMS is absorbed into the bloodstream and can circulate around the whole body. AMS is passed into the urine, making it smell foul, and can also pass through the skin, tainting your sweat. Any AMS that makes it to your lungs is exhaled as garlic breath. The whole process can take several days from the moment you eat the garlic.

As long as there has been garlic breath, there have been a variety of supposed remedies—but is there any scientific basis to suggest that any of these natural remedies actually work?

## Parsley

Eating fresh parsley is probably the cure that is most often mentioned. The reason is the supposed effect of chlorophyll, the green pigment found in plants. Parsley, which has a deep green color, contains high levels of chlorophyll, and as a result, it's often found in recipes containing a lot of garlic, including garlic bread. But what of parsley's effectiveness in scientific terms?

As far back as 1953, scientists have been contesting the efficacy of chlorophyll. In a paper called "Assessment of Chlorophyll as a Deodorant" in the *British Medical Journal*, Dr. John Brocklehurst of the University of Glasgow found that chlorophyll had no noticeable effect on the smell of garlic.

In the paper he writes: "Mixtures of water-soluble chlorophyll and various strong-smelling solutions [including syrup of garlic] did not remove the smell of these solutions even after exposure for one or more months."

## Other natural remedies

Many of the accepted traditional cures for garlic breath have no proven basis in scientific fact either. For example, chewing fennel seeds, anise, or cardamom is supposed to help cure garlic breath. Fennel seeds are often found in Indian restaurants for just this purpose. Yet there is no known scientific evidence to back this up.

It appears that it is really the strong smell of each of these remedies that masks the smell of garlic temporarily rather than neutralizing it in any chemical way.

## The scientific remedies

So what does work, according to the scientists? Quite simply, mouthwash. Often used for controlling bad breath generally, there is some evidence that certain types of mouthwash do combat garlic breath.

The Cochrane Collaboration, a not-for-profit network of researchers around the world, conducted a review of scientific evidence on the use of mouthwash to combat bad breath. It looked at five randomized controlled trials—in which test subjects were randomly given either a mouthwash or a similar placebo solution—to see if there was any overwhelming scientific evidence that they work.

This systematic review found that mouthwashes containing antibacterial agents, such as chlorhexidine and cetylpyridinium

chloride, "may play an important role in reducing the levels of halitosis-producing bacteria on the tongue," while those containing chlorine dioxide and zinc "can be effective in the neutralization of odoriferous sulfur compounds."

As odoriferous sulfur compounds go, AMS is among the most odoriferous. So next time you buy a bottle of mouthwash, look at the label to make sure it contains chlorine dioxide and zinc. And that, sadly, is the limit of our current armory in the scientific battle against garlic breath, apart from abstention.

# How to organize

As you grow older, you start building up large collections of things, particularly books, CDs, and DVDs. As your collections grow, locating what you want can become quite a challenge. Organizing items can be divided into two separate disciplines: sorting them initially and finding the item you want when you come to look for it.

## Bubble sort

Imagine you have the following collection of books that you want to organize alphabetically: *Quotations from Chairman Mao*; *Lord of the Flies*; *The Complete Works of William Shakespeare*; *The Times Atlas of the World*; the Bible (see Fig. 1 on the following page).

You can use something called a bubble sort to put them in order (so called because items that are out of order bubble up the list). Compare the first item to the second. If they are in the wrong order, change them; if not, leave them. Move to the second and third items and do the same. Continue until you reach the end of the list; if you haven't swapped any items, it is sorted; if you have, go back to the beginning and start again. Here's how it would go (using just the first initial of each title to make it easier to follow):

> **Q**L**C**TB ——> **L**Q**C**TB ——> LC**Q**TB (no change)
> ——> LC**Q**TB ——> LC**QB**T

Then back to the start again:

> **L**C**Q**BT ——> **C**L**Q**BT (no change) ——> CL**Q**BT
> ——> CL**BQ**T (no change) ——> CL**BQ**T

Then back to the start again:

> **C**L**B**QT (no change) ——> C**L**B**Q**T ——>
> CB**L**QT (no change) ——> CBL**Q**T (no change)

Continue going back to the start until you end up with:

**BCLQT** (no change) ——> **BCLQT** (no change) ——>
**BCLQT** (no change) ——> **BCLQT** (no change)

No changes have been made, so the books are in order.

You might also think that it is an incredibly time-consuming way of sorting, and you would be right. Algorithms are rated on their computational complexity—i.e., a measure of how long it will take to sort the list in the worst-case scenario. If the list has $n$ items and is completely out of order, the bubble sort requires $n - 1$ rounds and $n$ comparisons within each round. The total

Fig. 1 Bubble sorting your books

number of steps will be $(n - 1)$ times $n$ in the worst case or $n^2 - 2n + 1$. When $n$ is really large, the $n^2$ part of this is so large that it dominates the $2n$ and 1; if $n$ is 100, for example, then $n^2$ is 10,000, while $2n$ is just 200. The complexity is then said to be of the order of $n^2$ or $O(n^2)$.

## Quicksort

Now that we know the computational complexity of the bubble sort, we can look at other possible algorithms which might prove to be faster and easier. One of the fastest methods of sorting is known as quicksort, which was invented by the computer scientist Tony Hoare (now Sir Charles Antony Hoare) in 1960.

In the quicksort algorithm, you pick one element from your

list, called the pivot. You then reorder the list so that anything that has a lower number than the pivot or precedes it alphabetically is moved before the pivot; anything higher or that succeeds it alphabetically goes after. The chosen pivot will then be in the correct position in the list. You then reapply this to the individual sublists before and after the pivot, choosing a new pivot for each sublist until there is only one element left in the sublist. Let's see how it works with our list (the pivot at each stage is in bold):

Q**L**CTB ——> BCQLT

There is only one item in the sublist before C, which shows that both B and C are now in the correct position, so we look at the sublist to the right of C:

BC **Q**LT ——> BC LQT

Move Q after the pivot, and L is now in the correct position:

BCL **Q**T

Then we can see that the Q and T are already in the right place.

We have sorted our list. The quicksort has computational complexity of order ($n \log n$), where $\log n$ is the logarithm of the number $n$. As $n$ gets increasingly larger, $n \log n$ gets substantially smaller than $n^2$, which we know is the computational complexity of the bubble sort, showing us that the quicksort is more efficient than the bubble sort. If we have a collection of 1,000 DVDs to sort, the bubble sort has a complexity of order 1,000 x 1,000, or 1,000,000. So it might take around a million steps to sort it into correct order in the worst-case scenario. Quicksort has a complexity of order 1,000 x log 1,000, or 1,000 x 3 = 3,000. So it might take around 3,000 steps in the worst case to sort it into order. That's quite some time saving.

# Frequency filing

So much for sorting, what about finding? Generally, people will file and organize alphabetically, but that isn't necessarily always the best way.

Say you have a box or filing cabinet full of personal papers in your house that might include utility bills (U), your birth certificate (C), your bank statements (B), insurance documents (I), and stock certificates (S). When you are looking for a particular item, you probably start at the top of the box and move down, or start from the front of the filing cabinet and move back.

Let's imagine they are sorted alphabetically (BCISU). Let's say that it takes two minutes to go through and find each item that you need, i.e., two minutes to find the bank statement, four to find the birth certificate, and up to ten to find the utility bills.

If you access your stock certificates once a day, your bank statements once a week, your utility bills once a month, your insurance documents once a year, and your birth certificate once every ten years, then your searching time over your 50-year adult life will be:

$$
\begin{array}{ccc}
\text{B} & \text{C} & \text{S} \\
\end{array}
$$
$$
T = (50 \times 52 \times 2) + (5 \times 4) + (50 \times 6) +
$$
$$
\begin{array}{cc}
\text{I} & \text{U} \\
\end{array}
$$
$$
(50 \times 365 \times 8) + (50 \times 12 \times 10) = 157{,}520 \text{ minutes}
$$

Now look to see what happens if your personal documents are sorted instead by their frequency of use, i.e., SBUIC:

$$
\begin{array}{ccc}
\text{S} & \text{B} & \text{U} \\
\end{array}
$$
$$
T = (50 \times 365 \times 2) + (50 \times 52 \times 4) + (50 \times 12 \times 6) +
$$
$$
\begin{array}{cc}
\text{I} & \text{C} \\
\end{array}
$$
$$
(50 \times 8) + (5 \times 10) = 50{,}950 \text{ minutes}
$$

Just putting your documents into order of frequency has saved you 106,570 minutes or around 74 days during your adult life.

# How to make your food last longer

Have you ever wondered what makes food go bad? The thing that turns your fresh piece of fish into a stinking pulp in a matter of days (or hours, if you leave it out in the sun) is bacteria.

These microorganisms are present virtually everywhere on earth—in the soil and in the bodies of living plants and animals. Many are harmless but some can cause you to become ill if you eat them. And the more bacteria that are in the food you eat, the more likely it is that you will become ill.

Bacteria grow through cell division, with each bacterium dividing into two new ones. With a friendly, warm, and nutritious environment, a typical *E. coli* bacterium—responsible for one type of food poisoning—can divide into two every twenty minutes. After another twenty minutes, those two can divide into four. This doubling every twenty minutes causes a rapid growth in the number of bacteria. Over the course of twelve hours, a single bacterium can be transformed into a thriving colony of 68 billion of the little critters.

One obvious answer is to wash your hands before touching food (guess where many of those bacteria come from?), but is there anything else we can do? After all, food is so expensive and we're all concerned about all that packaging these days that fewer trips to the supermarket can't be a bad thing.

## Keep it cool

We all know that putting food in the fridge can help because the low temperature stops the bacteria from multiplying as quickly. Don't forget to keep it as cold as you can without making your milk freeze. Keep the door closed whenever possible—don't leave it open while pouring cream in your coffee, for example.

## Hands off

Not touching food at all can make it last longer. If you cut cheese, for instance, try to keep the plastic around it rather than holding it with your bare hand. On the subject of cheese, if it starts to develop moldy spots, don't eat those bits; they could be toxic. Rather than wasting the whole cheese, cut a cube about an inch around the spot and use the rest.

## The ethylene issue

Fruits and vegetables emit a gas called ethylene as part of their ripening process. The rate at which fruits and vegetables produce this colorless and odorless gas is governed by temperature. At very low temperatures, the production of ethylene virtually stops. This is why putting fruits and vegetables in a cool place, such as the fridge, slows down the ripening (and spoiling) process.

Some unexpected problems occur, however, when you put together food products that produce a lot of ethylene, such as tomatoes and bananas, with other products that are sensitive to ethylene, such as lettuce and broccoli.

The extra gas in the environment means that the latter ripen far faster than they would if they were stored on their own.

This is also the reason why you should remove fruits and vegetables as soon as possible once they have gone bad. Decaying fruits and vegetables produce higher concentrations of ethylene, causing the remaining fruits and vegetables to spoil even faster. It really is true that one bad apple spoils the bunch, as the proverb says.

## Mold control

It is not bacteria that make bread go bad but mold. Molds are a form of microscopic fungi, which are carried by the wind or vibration onto the surface of food. Once there, they grow by feasting on nutrients and moisture in the bread. As they grow, they develop spores, which detach and infect other parts of the bread.

air flows freely

Molds thrive in warm, moist conditions, and this poses a particular problem for conveniently sliced loaves stored in a plastic bag. Water remaining inside the bread evaporates and makes the surface of the loaf moist. The best way to store bread is in a dry and clean container that permits airflow, which stops the bread surface from becoming moist in the first place.

# How to save power

The high price of electricity and the increasing desire to go green and reduce carbon emissions mean that people are looking at how much electricity they use in their everyday lives more than ever before.

## Power-hungry appliances

Electricity consumption is measured in kilowatt hours (kWh). A 100-watt (the same as 0.1 kilowatt) light bulb used for an hour consumes 0.1 kWh of power; over ten hours, it consumes 1 kWh.

The average American household uses approximately 11,040 kilowatt hours (kWh) of electricity every year. The average figure hides wide variations: the average consumption in Tennessee in 2008 was 15,624 kWh while in Maine it was 6,252 kWh. At the time of writing, the average retail price of electricity was 10.54 cents per kWh.

Different appliances and devices use widely different amounts of electricity to operate. Once you know the appliances that use the most electricity, you can start to see where you could try to save power. Clearly the easiest method is simply to turn off appliances when you are not using them, but knowing a little bit of science means that you can also use some of your appliances in a more energy-efficient way.

The following table gives average energy consumption figures for US households.

| Appliance/device | Annual power consumption (kWh) per appliance |
|---|---|
| Space heater | 3,524* |
| Central air conditioning | 2,796* |
| Water heater | 2,552* |
| Pool heater | 2,300 |
| Pool pump | 1,500 |
| Refrigerator | 1,239 |
| Freezer | 1,039 |
| Lighting | 940* |
| Electric range top | 536 |
| Dishwasher | 512* |
| Electric oven | 440 |
| Desktop PC | 262 |
| Multi-function printer | 216 |
| Microwave oven | 209 |
| Television | 137 |
| Washing machine | 120 |
| Coffee maker | 116 |
| Compact stereo system | 81 |
| Laptop computer | 77 |
| DVD player | 70 |

Source: US Energy Information Administration.     Note: * Per household not per unit

## Power cycles

You can see from the table above that refrigerators and freezers are among the most power-hungry of appliances in the typical home. However, refrigerators and freezers do not consume power evenly. Unlike a tea kettle, which might consume 2kW of power for the entire five minutes it is on, a fridge uses power in cycles. So if the thermostat on your fridge is set to 43°F (6°C), and the temperature in the fridge rises above this, the cooling circuits kick in and the fridge starts to consume large amounts of energy.

Coolant passes around the system absorbing heat from the fridge compartment and then dumping this heat into the room in which it is standing. As soon as the temperature is below 43°F (6°C), the cooling stops and the power consumption falls to a trickle.

We can use this knowledge to our advantage. The frequency that the fridge cooling circuits operates depends strongly on the room temperature; they use far more electricity in summer than in winter, for example. So if we set our home's thermostat down by a degree, we not only save electricity on our heating bill but also give the fridge a break.

It also highlights the benefit of keeping the door to the refrigerator closed as much as possible. Every time you leave the door open, warm air from the room passes inside and the cooling circuits have to start again. When you are pouring a glass of orange juice, close the fridge door while you are doing it.

The typical power consumption of refrigerators has fallen dramatically in the past four decades. A pre-1976 fridge was using an average of 1,800 kWh a year. By 1990, it was half this and by 2001, it was almost a quarter. Today's energy efficient refrigerator freezers use around 200 to 300 kWh. If you have an old fridge, replacing it will dramatically cut your energy consumption and, potentially, save you money over the long term, offsetting the cost of replacing the fridge.

## Specific heat capacity

In practice, tea kettles are hugely power-hungry. A modern, fast-boiling kettle uses 3 kilowatts of power. However, since it boils in a couple of minutes, the total consumption is relatively low. Yet you can still reduce this figure by filling the kettle carefully (see Fig. 1).

The amount of heat (and therefore power) required to raise water to boiling point is proportional to the volume of water used. A property called the specific heat capacity tells us that it requires around 0.00116 kWh of energy to raise the temperature of a liter of water by 1°C. That means that the power used in boiling four cups' worth of water is four times the power used in boiling one cup. Filling your kettle with just the amount of water you need will therefore save power.

This same physical property of water can also help us save power when using the washing machine. Much of the electricity used by a washing machine is used in raising the temperature of the water. The amount of energy required is proportional to the temperature difference between the incoming water and the wash temperature. If the water coming into the machine is at 68°F (20°C), then running the machine at 140°F (60°C) takes twice as much power as running it at 104°F (40°C).

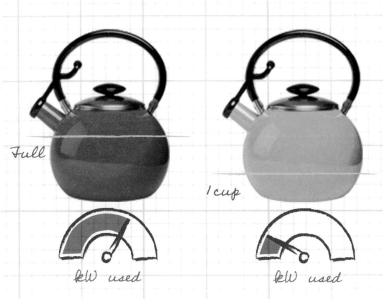

Fig. 1 Saving power by filling the tea kettle carefully

# How to neutralize smells

Whether due to pets, spills, or a pair of old and particularly malodorous running shoes, our homes can sometimes suffer from unpleasant smells, and getting rid of them permanently can present somewhat of a challenge.

## The science of smell

The sense of smell is actually a broad name for a very complicated set of chemical-induced interactions that take place inside your nose. Smelly things, such as flowers, foods, and fragrances, give off chemicals, either through the process of evaporation or through the wind blowing molecules from their surfaces. These chemicals can drift into your nostrils, allowing you to smell them.

Inside your nose are millions of things called olfactory receptor neurons, which you can think of as sockets with different shapes. Among those millions, there are probably around 350 differently shaped sockets.

The aromatic chemical that enters your nose as an oddly-shaped plug only fits into the correctly shaped socket. When it reaches the socket, the neuron sends an electrical signal to the brain, enabling you to recognize it.

The process does not stop there. Most smells are actually complicated combinations of chemicals. The smell of coffee is made up of more than 800 different aromatic compounds, and when the coffee aroma enters the nose, it is a combination of different sockets that get plugged. It is the various combinations of sockets—and therefore signals to the brain—that allow us to distinguish one smell from another. Through these combinations, we can recognize around 10,000 different smells.

## Masking odors

The complex nature of smells makes neutralizing them a challenge. Household air fresheners are usually little more than pleasant-smelling perfumes. Spraying them in a room where there is an odor of animal urine or cooked fish does nothing to neutralize the odors themselves. Instead, the smell of the air freshener is designed to overpower the stench of the bad-smelling chemicals. This is why they often use pungent scents, such as pine and lemon.

What comes as a surprise to lots of people is that many air fresheners contain mild anesthetics, such as formaldehyde. Instead of neutralizing the odor itself, these numb your sense of smell.

Air-freshening devices often use something called activated carbon filters to remove bad smells. Activated carbon is carbon (perhaps in the form of charcoal) that has been processed to make it extremely porous. The network of holes in the carbon provides an enormous surface area—a single gram of activated carbon can have a surface area between 500 and 1,500 square meters. It is this surface area that is key to neutralizing smells. Molecules of the smell in question get stuck to this extended surface through a process known as absorption.

## The natural solution

If you don't want to use a commercial air freshener, there are alternatives. Baking soda, which is used by cooks to help make dough and cakes rise, is very good at absorbing pungent smells. It is also useful for spills of smelly liquids, since it is very good at absorbing moisture.

Vinegar is another simple product you can find in the kitchen that can reduce smells. Distilled white vinegar is a dilute solution of ethanoic acid (also called acetic acid), and its chemical reactions with other substances can help remove odors. For example, the smell of urine is caused in part by the chemical ammonia. Ethanoic acid and ammonia can neutralize each other, leaving just salts and water.

# How to win at pool

The best pool players in the world are those that know a great deal about science. They may not know the exact equations that govern the movement of the balls as they collide with each other and with the sides of the table, but they know instinctively what will happen when they release their cue. Winning at pool is all about knowing the conservation of momentum and energy.

## Using the conservation of momentum and energy

Momentum, the "desire" of an object to keep on moving, is very well-defined in physics. It is an object's mass (which most people would recognize as its weight) multiplied by its velocity. An object with a large mass and/or a high velocity has a high momentum and is difficult to slow down. An object with low mass and/or low velocity—and therefore low momentum—is easier to slow down.

Momentum plays a very important role in collisions between objects, such as the balls on a pool table. For example, when you hit the cue ball, the force of your shot transfers momentum to the cue ball. If this hits another ball, some or all of that momentum is transferred to the other ball.

Let's look at the situation where the cue ball hits the red ball head on. This means the collision is simple, and we can replace the velocity with the speed in the calculation of momentum. Let's say that the cue ball has a speed of $s_{C1}$ before the collision and $s_{C2}$ after, and the red ball $s_{R1}$ before and $s_{R2}$ after.

The law of conservation of momentum tells us that the total momentum of the two balls before the collision is equal to it afterward. We assume that both balls have the same mass, $m$.

$$ms_{C1} + ms_{R1} = ms_{C2} + ms_{R2}$$

Dividing everything by $m$ gives us:

$$s_{C1} + s_{R1} = s_{C2} + s_{R2}$$
(equation A)

The law of conservation of energy also applies. The energy due to the motion of an object, known as the kinetic energy, is given by $\frac{1}{2}ms^2$. The total before the collision is the same after so we can write:

$$\frac{1}{2}ms_{C1}^2 + \frac{1}{2}ms_{R1}^2 = \frac{1}{2}ms_{C2}^2 + \frac{1}{2}ms_{R2}^2$$

Dividing everything by $m$ gives us:

$$s_{C1}^2 + s_{R1}^2 = s_{C2}^2 + s_{R2}^2$$
(equation B)

If we consider the situation you come across in pool where the ball you are aiming at is stationary (i.e., $s_{R1}=0$) we can simplify equations A and B as follows:

$$s_{C1} = s_{C2} + s_{R2}$$
(equation C)

and

$$s_{C1}^2 = s_{C2}^2 + s_{R2}^2$$
(equation D)

If we square both sides of equation C, we get

$$s_{C1}^2 = (s_{C2} + s_{R2})(s_{C2} + s_{R2}) = s_{C2}^2 + s_{R2}^2 + 2\,s_{C2}\,s_{R2}$$
(equation E)

But if you compare equations D and E, you'll notice that the only difference is the "$2 \, s_{C2} \, s_{R2}$" term at the very end. This must therefore be equal to zero, and if that's the case then either $s_{R2}$ or $s_{C2}$ must be zero.

## The theory in practice

The case of $s_{R2}$ equal to zero refers to the situation immediately before the collision; while the case of $s_{C2}$ equal to zero refers to the situation immediately after the collision. This latter case is interesting. It tells us that the cue ball has zero velocity after the collision—i.e., it is stationary. If this is the case, what happens to the red ball? Plugging $s_{C2}=0$ into equation C, shows us that $s_{R2} = s_{C1}$—i.e., the red ball moves off with the same velocity that the cue ball had initially.

This matches our experience of pool well although we would also have to consider the friction on the balls from the felt. Some additional energy is lost in the collision, some of which we hear as that satisfying click of balls.

The same idea can be used to consider the case of two pool balls hitting each other in a glancing collision rather than head on, although in this case we would have to take into account the vector nature of velocity since the collision would no longer be one-dimensional. Now that there are angles involved we would have to move into two dimensions and consider velocity's vector characteristics—a quantity with direction as well as size. The science involved is necessarily more in depth.

## Considering angles

Take a look at the game of pool in the diagram below (Fig. 1). The cue ball is labeled *c* and there's a black ball labeled *b*.

Clearly, if we want to sink the black ball we need to make sure that the angle represented by the Greek letter *theta* is just right to make the black ball's arrow point in the direction of the pocket. In this example the angle is actually a right angle, or 90 degrees. So how do we use this knowledge?

To actually sink the ball, imagine a line drawn from the center of the black ball to the pocket (labeled *a*). Then imagine the cue ball at the point of contact with the black ball (labeled *b*). We can then work out the direction the cue ball needs to travel to reach this point. To control the angle of the cue ball, you move the cue to the left of the center of the ball if you want it to travel to the right and vice versa. If you want it to travel straight forward (in

*Fig. 1: The correct angle to sink the ball in the pocket*

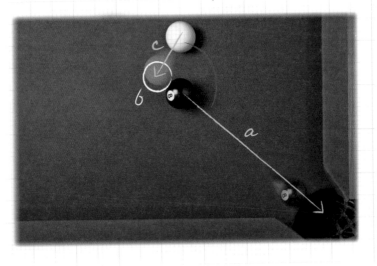

*Fig. 2: The correct angle to hit the ball using the cushion*

order to clip the ball into a side pocket perhaps), then just hit the cue ball dead in the center.

## Using cushions

Another use of physics is determining how balls bounce off cushions. Again we can use the law of conservation of momentum. If we assume that the collision with the cushion is elastic—i.e., no kinetic energy is lost—then we can show that the ball will bounce off the cushion just like a laser beam bouncing off a mirror—i.e., the incoming angle (shown by the *a*) is equal to the outgoing angle (shown by *b*) as shown in the diagram above (Fig. 2).

This proves incredibly useful when you are stuck behind another ball. If you know the angle, you can aim to avoid the blocking ball and hit your target ball.

# How to win at card games

Lady Luck is often invoked when playing card games, but the truth of the matter is that success has more to do with probability. More specifically, if you know everything there is to know about the probability of turning over certain cards, then the odds are dramatically improved in your favor.

## Playing with probability

The probability of some event happening—for example, drawing a particular card—is given by dividing the number of successful events by the number of possible events. Imagine you have a deck of 52 cards. What is the probability of drawing an ace from it?

**Probability of drawing an ace =**

$$\frac{\text{aces in deck}}{\text{cards in deck}} = \frac{4}{52} = 0.077 \text{ or } 7.7\%$$

When combining probabilities, we multiply them together if they are dependent and add them if they are independent.

So, since there are three aces remaining in the deck, which now comprises 51 cards after the first one has been removed, the probability of then picking a second ace from the deck is:

$$\frac{4}{52} \times \frac{3}{51} = 0.0045 = 0.45\%$$

Whereas if we want to know the probability of drawing an ace or a two in a full deck, we add the two probabilities:

$$\text{Probability of an ace OR a two} =$$
$$\frac{4}{52} + \frac{4}{52} = 0.154 \text{ or } 15.4\%$$

## Blackjack basics

We can apply this to help us determine our chances of winning card games. For example, what is the probability of being dealt a blackjack? The first card must be an ace and the other one must be one of the 16 cards in a deck worth ten (a 10, jack, queen, or king from one of the four suits) or the other way around. We write this in probability terms as

$$\frac{4}{52} \times \frac{16}{51} + \frac{16}{52} \times \frac{4}{51} = 0.048 = 4.8\%$$

The probability of you getting dealt a blackjack is therefore 4.8 percent.

## Developing a playing strategy

In the real world of playing blackjack, what we want to do is translate probabilities into a playing strategy—i.e., knowing when to hit and when to stand.

Rather than having to work out all of the probabilities ourselves, some statisticians have done it for us. In the September 1956 edition of the *Journal of the American Statistical Association*, R. Baldwin and colleagues published a paper outlining the optimum strategy to take in blackjack involving a single deck of cards (the probabilities and course of action you should take will vary if more than one pack of cards is being used).

The table below shows what to do. Look at the dealer's upcard—the one that is showing—and then look at the total of your own cards. If you have one or more aces in your hand, use the bottom (soft) row. Otherwise, use the top (hard) row.

The figure in the column of the dealer's upcard shows the minimum total you should stand on—i.e., if your total is that number or less, then you should hit, otherwise you should stand.

| Dealer's upcard | | | | | | | | | | |
|---|---|---|---|---|---|---|---|---|---|---|
| | 2 | 3 | 4 | 5 | 6 | 7 | 8 | 9 | 10 | 1, 11 |
| Minimum standing number (hard) | 13 | 13 | 12 | 12 | 12 | 17 | 17 | 17 | 17 | 17 |
| Minimum standing number (soft) | 18 | 18 | 18 | 18 | 18 | 18 | 18 | 17 | 17 | 18 |

# Texas hold 'em

In Texas hold 'em, each player is dealt two cards face down—the hole cards. Five community cards are then dealt face up in the middle—a set of three known as the flop, a fourth known as the turn and a fifth known as the river. Betting can take place before the flop, before the turn and before the river community cards are dealt.

The aim of the game is to get the best hand of five cards from the seven in total, according to the usual ranking of hands in poker: straight flush, four of a kind, full house, flush, straight, three of a kind, two pair, one pair, high card.

## Probabilities and outs

Probability can be used to assess the cards that are still in the deck that could complete a desired hand (these cards are known as outs). For example, you might have two hearts in your hand and two hearts and a diamond in the flop. You can use probability to work out the chances of a heart being dealt at the turn or river, which would complete a flush. Since there are nine other hearts remaining (13 minus the two in your hand and two in the flop) then the probability of getting one on the turn is 9/47 or 0.1915 or a 19.15 percent chance. The chance of getting one on the river if you didn't on the turn is 9/46 or 0.1957 or a 19.57 percent chance.

The chances for a getting a winning hand for various numbers of outs is shown in the table below, all of which have been calculated in the same way. To use it just think how many cards remain in the deck that could complete your hand. For example,

| Outs | Chances of completing hand on turn (T) = outs/47 | Chances of completing hand on river (R) = outs/46 | Chances of completing hand on turn OR river = 100%–(100–T) x (100–R)) |
|---|---|---|---|
| 1 | 2.13% | 2.17% | 4.26% |
| 2 | 4.26% | 4.35% | 8.42% |
| 3 | 6.38% | 6.52% | 12.49% |
| 4 | 8.51% | 8.70% | 16.47% |
| 5 | 10.64% | 10.87% | 20.35% |
| 6 | 12.77% | 13.04% | 24.14% |
| 7 | 14.89% | 15.22% | 27.84% |
| 8 | 17.02% | 17.39% | 31.45% |
| 9 | 19.15% | 19.57% | 34.97% |
| 10 | 21.28% | 21.74% | 38.39% |
| 11 | 23.40% | 23.91% | 41.72% |
| 12 | 25.53% | 26.09% | 44.96% |
| 13 | 27.66% | 28.26% | 48.10% |
| 14 | 29.79% | 30.43% | 51.16% |
| 15 | 31.91% | 32.61% | 54.12% |
| 16 | 34.04% | 34.78% | 56.98% |
| 17 | 36.17% | 36.96% | 59.76% |
| 18 | 38.30% | 39.13% | 62.44% |
| 19 | 40.43% | 41.30% | 65.03% |
| 20 | 42.55% | 43.48% | 67.53% |

if there are three aces in your hand and the flop, there is only one possible remaining ace that could complete the hand; the number of outs is therefore 1 and the chances of you getting the ace in either the turn OR the river is 4.26 percent.

## Twos and fours

A simple way of estimating these figures during a game is the rule of two and four: You will notice that the percentages in the first two columns are close to the number of outs multiplied by 2 while the percentages in the last column are close to the number of outs multiplied by 4. We call these percentages the card odds.

The next thing to do is work out the pot odds, the ratio of your opponent's last bet to the total pot. If there is $100 in the pot and the bet is $10, then the pot odds are $10/$100, or 10 percent. If your card odds (i.e., the chances of getting a winning hand) are much higher than the pot odds, then it's probably a good idea to call (i.e., match your opponent's bet). Otherwise, you should fold.

The odds are always in favor of the house, but perhaps a little knowledge of math and probability can increase your chances, or at least reduce your losses!

# How to get a lid off a jar

Storing food in glass jars has been a practice for more than two centuries and it was French emperor Napoleon's need to feed his armies that made it a success. Bottling food in jars was pioneered by the French confectioner Nicholas Appert in 1795 and the idea won him a 12,000 franc prize from Napoleon, who is often quoted as saying, "An army marches on its stomach."

Appert's jars worked well because of the method used to seal them. Each jar was filled with food and a small air space was left at the top. He would then seal the jar with cork and sealing wax before boiling the jar in water, cooking whatever was inside.

## The vacuum seal

The beauty of the method is that the cooking process forces the air at the top of the food out of the jar. When the food cools, the

air contracts and forms a partial vacuum. The vacuum has a double benefit: it seals the lid very tightly and stops organisms that could spoil the food from getting in. It also means there is less oxygen inside the jar, something which most bacteria need to thrive.

The partial vacuum has an unfortunate side effect—it can make the lid extremely difficult to remove. But there are several different methods we can try.

## The water method

Run hot water from a faucet over the lid of the jar. Different materials—such as metal and glass—expand at different rates as the temperature rises, and the metal expands slightly faster than the glass. This means that the lid ever so gradually moves away from the jar, enabling you to remove it easily (see Fig. 1).

There is also a second physical effect going on. The metal of the lid has a much higher thermal conductivity than the glass, meaning the whole lid heats up very quickly compared to the glass.

*Fig. 1 Using hot water to expand the lid*

The water method is also useful if the jar has been opened previously and all that is stopping it is a buildup of food in the thread of the lid, as sometimes happens with a jar of honey. The additional heat can soften the congealed food.

## The tapping method

The vacuum can be broken in another way. Take a sturdy knife, like a butter knife, and tap it at several points around the lid. The taps will deform the lid slightly or weaken the seal enough to allow more air to enter the jar, letting you open it more easily.

## The friction method

Most jar lids are made of smooth metal, making it virtually impossible to get a good grip on the lid to twist it off. You need to increase the friction between your hand and the lid, allowing you to form a better grip.

Rubber is a non-slip material so if you have a pair of rubber gloves handy, put them on and try opening the lid. If you don't have rubber gloves, try placing a wide rubber band around the edge of the lid, or use a rough tea towel.

## The wait-a-while method

If you're having trouble opening a jar early in the morning, you might have more success if you can wait until later in the day. People's muscles are usually weaker in the morning after they have first woken up. If you had been drinking alcohol the night before, your muscles will also be dehydrated and not as strong.

## The fluid hammer method

This is not as drastic as it sounds and doesn't involve a hammer. Instead, hold the jar in the hand that you don't write with. Slap the bottom of the jar forcefully with your other hand (see Fig. 2). The fluid hammer effect causes the food inside the jar to slide up against the lid, releasing the lid a little and allowing a little air to enter, making the lid easier to remove.

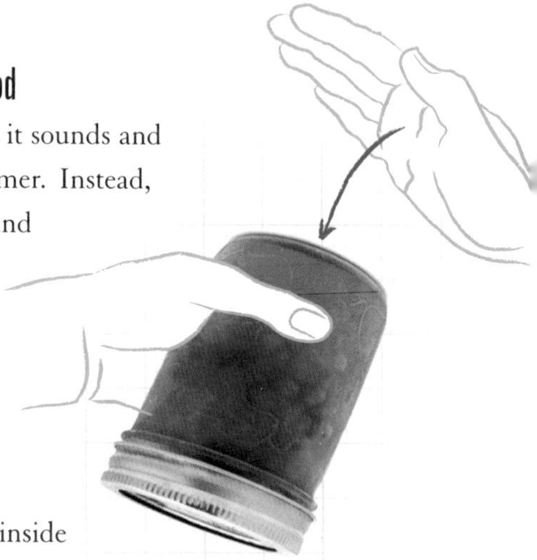

Fig. 2 Slapping the jar to release the lid

# How to win at the carnival

When you visited the carnival as a child, did you ever have the feeling that those kids wandering around with the big cuddly toys they had won were actually stooges paid by the carnival owner? Me too.

In fact, carnivals are little more than legalized scams and many of their sideshow games have been contrived to make it almost impossible to win. But then again, they give everyone a little entertainment and surely we should all be happy to pay for that. And there are some games that you stand a chance of winning, while others you shouldn't bother trying.

## Avoid completely

Games where you have to throw a basketball into a hoop should be avoided. The hoop is often oval rather than circular and it is impossible to get the ball through it. The oval shape isn't visible to you because of the optical illusion that makes circles appear elongated when viewed at an angle.

## Using the conservation of momentum

The real science of carnival trickery is evident in throwing games. First up is the stack of cans. Here the idea is to knock all the cans off a shelf to win a prize. The problem is that some of the cans—usually three along the bottom—are heavier than those on the top. The scientific law of conservation of momentum says that the weight and velocity of projectiles is related to the weight and velocity of the object hit by the projectile. A light ball traveling slowly before it hits a heavier object will only be able to

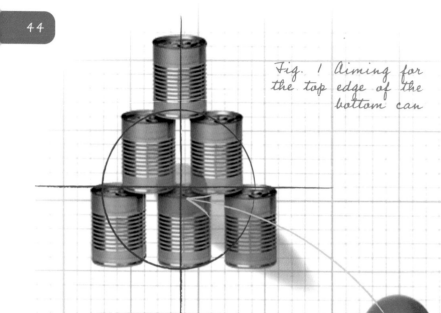

Fig. 1 Aiming for the top edge of the bottom can

make the object move more slowly than the ball. If you do play, focus your attention on hitting the top edges of the bottom cans and throwing the ball as hard as you can (see Fig. 1). This is your only real chance of success.

## Finding the right angle

Hoopla is almost impossible to win. The hoops are only just large enough to fit over most of the objects and the base is often covered with material so that the hoop has trouble slipping over it. Often the attendant will give a demonstration of how to win, showing that the hoop is able to fit over the base, to dispel any ideas that it might have been fixed. The truth is that the attendant knows exactly the angle at which a hoop can be placed over the base, so the best technique is to ask for a demonstration, preferably involving a thrown hoop, and watch carefully to see at what angle it needs to be to fit over. The bases with money attached to them should be avoided. They are the highest value prizes and therefore are the hardest to win.

## Trial and error

We all know about rifle ranges. No matter how well you align the sights, you always miss. This is because the sights are often misaligned for that very reason. Use your first shot to make a guess of how misaligned the sights are, and then use that to adjust your aim.

## Laws of deflection

Another carnival scam that uses the laws of physics is the ball-in-a-bucket game. You throw a ball and if it lands and stays in the bucket you win a prize. The trouble is that the bucket has been angled so that the balls usually bounce out again—in the same way that light bounces off a mirror. The bottom of the bucket is often surprisingly springy too.

You can also use physics to beat this game. Throw the ball with as little speed as possible. The collision with the bottom of the bucket absorbs some of its energy and the ball may not have enough energy left over to bounce back out. Giving the ball a little spin can also help because it makes the impact on the bottom of the bucket less predictable, meaning the ball can bounce off and hit the sides of the bucket.

So next time someone says to you "fair's fair," you can argue that it isn't—but that you don't really mind.

# How to win at Risk and other dice games

The board game Risk, in which competing armies try to take over groups of continents or the entire world, has been around for more than 50 years and has become one of the most popular strategic games among people of all ages. After you have been playing for a while, you begin to realize there are certain strategies you can adopt to improve your chance of success.

Players of the board game Risk roll dice against each other to mimic the effect of battles between their armies on the board.

The player whose turn it is can choose to attack a player in a neighboring country. The attacker can play between one and three dice (as long as this is one less than the number of attacking armies) while the defender can choose to roll one or two dice in response (limited to the number of defending armies in the country).

After the dice are rolled, they are placed in descending order for each player. The attacking player wins the battle between two armies if his dice roll is higher than the defender's dice roll for the corresponding army. The defender wins in the event of a tie.

## Analyzing the probabilities

There are, of course, a number of different strategies which you can employ during the game, but here we will focus on the role of the dice. The outcome of battles is governed by simple probability. Let's take a look at a single dice roll.

|  |  | Attacker rolls | | | | | |
|---|---|---|---|---|---|---|---|
|  |  | 1 | 2 | 3 | 4 | 5 | 6 |
| Defender rolls | 1 | D | A | A | A | A | A |
|  | 2 | D | D | A | A | A | A |
|  | 3 | D | D | D | A | A | A |
|  | 4 | D | D | D | D | A | A |
|  | 5 | D | D | D | D | D | A |
|  | 6 | D | D | D | D | D | D |

D = defender wins; A = attacker wins

For each battle, there are 36 possible outcomes, as shown in the table above. However, the defender wins in 21 of them, giving the defender a 21/36 or 58.3 percent chance of winning an individual battle. This seems to give the defender an unfair advantage. Yet the fact that an attacker can roll three dice to the defender's two evens out the odds.

The table on the next page gives the full probabilities for each type of battle. You can see that the 58.3 percent figure we worked out above is the second figure in the first column. Note that probabilities have to add up to 100 percent for any battle—it is certain that someone will win (although the figures do not always do so because of rounding errors).

| | | | Attacker | | |
|---|---|---|---|---|---|
| | | | One die | Two dice | Three dice |
| Defender | One die | Attacker wins | 41.7% | 57.9% | 66.0% |
| | | Defender wins | 58.3% | 42.1% | 34.0% |
| | Two Dice | Attacker wins | 25.5% | 22.8% | 37.2% |
| | | Defender wins | 74.5% | 44.8% | 29.3% |
| | | Both win one | — | 32.4% | 33.6% |

## Applying a strategy

So if you are playing a game of Risk and you can clearly work out all of the possible outcomes of the battles, as the attacker you can see when probability is working in your favor: you can assess whether the risk to your troops is worth attacking for, or if you should wait for a more advantageous situation. It is clearly always to the attacker's advantage to roll three dice—i.e., the probabilities that you will win are higher percentages. (The only exception to this is where you are fighting over a country that is at a dead end. Since you have to move the number of winning armies, you might end up with armies stuck in a country where you can't use them for future battles.)

If you compare the probabilities for defender wins in the second table, you can see that it is better to roll two dice rather than one where possible. Even though the probability for the defender winning is lower with two dice than one when the attacker rolls three, the average army wins per roll are higher. Or, look at it like this. Let's assume the attacker rolls three dice. If the defender rolls one die, there is only one army at stake. Since the probability is 66 percent that the attacker wins, the defender loses an average of 0.66 armies per dice roll.

If the defender rolls two dice, there are two armies at stake. Therefore the average armies lost by the defender over the two rolls is 37.2% x 2 (the attacker wins both) + 33.6% x 1 (the attacker wins one) or 1.08. Over one roll the figure is half this— 0.54 armies per dice roll—so the defender should roll two dice to lose the least number of armies on average per dice roll.

## Probabilities in other dice games

Analyzing the probable outcomes is a method that can be employed in other dice-based games as well, for example in the casino game of craps. In craps, the shooter places a bet in one of two places, called the Pass line and the Don't Pass line, and rolls two dice. Shooters play against the house.

The first roll of the dice is called the come-out roll, and if the shooter scores 7 or 11, the game is over. Any bets placed on the Pass line win (the shooter gets twice the bet back) while those on the Don't Pass line lose.

A come-out roll of 2, 3, or 12 is called "craps" and the game is also over. This time, bets on the Pass line lose and those on the Don't Pass line win.

For any other come-out roll (4, 5, 6, 8, 9, or 10), this figure becomes known as the point. The shooter then continues rolling. If he rolls the same figure again, the game is over and bets on the Pass line win and bets on the Don't Pass line lose. If the shooter rolls a 7, the game is over and bets on the Pass line lose while those on the Don't Pass line win. For any other roll, the game continues.

The table shows all the possible totals of the two dice rolled by the shooter.

| | | Die 1 | | | | | |
|---|---|---|---|---|---|---|---|
| | | 1 | 2 | 3 | 4 | 5 | 6 |
| Die 2 | 1 | 2 | 3 | 4 | 5 | 6 | 7 |
| | 2 | 3 | 4 | 5 | 6 | 7 | 8 |
| | 3 | 4 | 5 | 6 | 7 | 8 | 9 |
| | 4 | 5 | 6 | 7 | 8 | 9 | 10 |
| | 5 | 6 | 7 | 8 | 9 | 10 | 11 |
| | 6 | 7 | 8 | 9 | 10 | 11 | 12 |

The table shows there are 36 possible outcomes, and that there are six ways of throwing 7. Therefore the probability of throwing 7 is 6/36, or 1/6, which works out to 16.66 percent. Similarly, the probability of throwing an 11 is 2/36, or 1/18, which is 5.55 percent.

You can also work out the possibility of throwing 4, 5, 6, 8, 9, or 10 on the come-out roll and then the same number again before you throw a 7. Adding all these together, gives an overall chance of winning a bet on the Pass line as 49.29 percent. This means that the casino wins the rest of the time, or 50.71 percent of the time. On a typical bet of $100, you will lose around $1.42. Whereas on the Don't Pass line, if you work out the probability of shooting a 2, 3, or a 12 and taking into account that you only get your stake back if a 12 is rolled (rather than double), you can show that the average loss per $100 bet is around $1.40.

So what has this taught us about playing this particular game? That the casino always wins (although you lose less if you bet on the Don't Pass line), so it might be better to pass on this game.

# How to solve newspaper logic puzzles

Have you ever looked at the puzzle page in a newspaper or magazine, or an advertisement to join the high IQ society Mensa, and been totally perplexed? Welcome to the world of logic puzzles. Knowing a little math, however, could help you solve them.

## Number sequences

Logic puzzles come in many shapes and sizes but most of them have one thing in common—they usually present a list of numbers or objects, and you are asked to guess the next one.

For example, you might be asked to work out the next number in the following list of numbers:

1    3    6    10    15    21    28    ...

## Using math to solve number sequences

Rather than wasting your time making a guess at what the next item in a sequence is, you need to use different types of mathematical techniques to crack them.

Number sequences like the example above usually take the form of what mathematicians call an arithmetic progression or sequence, in which the difference between any two successive numbers is the same. The sequence 2, 4, 6, 8, 10, 12, and so forth is an arithmetic progression because each term is two larger than the previous one.

We can work out what the next number should be by calculating the successive differences between consecutive numbers in the sequence, and the best way to do this is by writing down the numbers in the sequence in a pyramid as shown below. The line below shows the difference between each.

$$1 \quad 3 \quad 6 \quad 10 \quad 15 \quad 21 \quad 28 \quad \ldots$$
$$2 \quad 3 \quad 4 \quad 5 \quad 6 \quad 7$$

Very quickly you can see the underlying sequence. The difference between successive numbers increases by one every time. Knowing this, we can see that the difference between our highest number 28 and the next should be 8, giving $28+8 = 36$.

We can show this regular increase in the sequence in an equation that you could use to work out any number further along in the sequence, without needing to work out all the ones in between. Numbers in an arithmetic sequence take the standard mathematical form.

$$a_n = a_1 + (n - 1)d$$

What this means is that the $n$th number in the sequence (which we call $a_n$) is equal to the first number in the sequence ($a_1$) plus the standard difference, $d$, multiplied by $n$ minus one. In our 2, 4, 6, 8, 10, 12 sequence we can see that $a_1 = 2$ and that $d = 2$. So with this formula we can calculate $a_3$ to be 6.

More generally we can see that an arithmetic sequence will look like this:

$$a_1 \quad a_1 + d \quad a_1 + 2d \quad a_1 + 3d \text{ and so on}$$

If we do what we did above and write out a pyramid of successive differences we can see:

$$a_1 \quad a_1 + d \quad a_1 + 2d \quad a_1 + 3d$$
$$d \qquad d \qquad d$$

This demonstrates why the successive differences method works to solve easy arithmetic sequences.

So if you wanted to work out the 10th number in the sequence, put the numbers into the equation and you can see that it would come out as 20.

## Tackling advanced sequences

Here's a different type of sequence:

1    2    6    15    31    56    ...

If we use the successive difference method, we get:

1    2    6    15    31    56    ...
   1    4    9    16    25

Here you can see that the difference is not the same number each time. However, there is still a pattern, but it is still not that obvious (unless you happen to know the squares of the first five numbers are 1, 4, 9, 16, and 25). We can take the pyramid idea down one more level and compare differences between the second line:

1    2    6    15    31    56    ...
   1    4    9    16    25
      3    5    7    9

You should be able to see that this is the sequence of odd numbers and that the next number in the bottom line should be 11, meaning the next number in the second line should be 25+11, or 36. This means the next number in the top line is 56+36, or 92.

Again, this can be expressed as an equation to work out any number in the sequence. If we look at our second, more complex example, we see that each term can be written mathematically as:

$$a_n = a_{n-1} + (n - 1)^2$$

(If you try this with $n$ = 1, 2, 3, etc., you will see that's correct.)

So by adding an extra 1 to $n$ at each stage, we get the next number in our sequence, which we can write as:

$$a_n+1 = a_n + n^2$$
$$a_{n+2} = a_{n+1} + (n + 1)^2$$

The typical difference between the two consecutive terms (i.e., the second line of our pyramid) is therefore written as:

$$a_{n+1} - a_n = a_n + n^2 - a_n = n^2$$

Apply the same to $a_{n+2}$:

$$a_{n+2} - a_{n+1} = a_{n+1} + (n + 1)^2 - a_n - n^2$$
$$= a_n + n^2 + (n + 1)^2 - a_n - n^2 = n^2 + 2n + 1$$

So the difference between these two terms gives us the third row of our pyramid:

$$\textbf{Difference} = n^2 + 2n + 1 - n^2 = 2n + 1$$

The $2n+1$ sequence is the sequence of odd numbers (try it with $n$ = 1, 2, 3 to check) and we can easily recognize this.

## Number squares

Another type of logic puzzle is number squares. You might be presented with a box containing several numbers as on the opposite page.

| ? | 9 | 2 |
|---|---|---|
| 3 | 5 | ? |
| 8 | ? | 6 |

You are told that each row and column adds up to the same number, and that the square contains each of the numbers 1 to 9 only once. Your job is to figure out the missing numbers.

## Using math to solve number squares

The number square we have been presented with is what mathematicians call a magic square, and the number each row and column adds up to is fixed according to the size of the square in question. They add up to the magic constant.

The total is as follows:

| Square size | Rows/columns add up to |
|---|---|
| 2 x 2 | 5 |
| 3 x 3 | 15 |
| 4 x 4 | 34 |
| 5 x 5 | 65 |
| 6 x 6 | 111 |
| 7 x 7 | 175 |
| 8 x 8 | 260 |

Since the square we are presented with in the first part of this chapter is 3 x 3, each row must add up to 15. Therefore the missing numbers are 4 (in the top row), 7 (in the second row), and 1 (in the last).

## The equation

The rows, columns, and diagonals of *n* x *n* magic squares all add up to what is known as the magic constant (*M*), and it is fairly straightforward to calculate from the following:

$$M = \frac{n(n^2 + 1)}{2}$$

The number in the middle square of an odd-sided magic square is always the same too—a three-sided square always has the number 5 at its center. In fact the middle square for an *n* x *n* square is always given by

$$Middle = \frac{(n^2 + 1)}{2}$$

Knowing this we can remember the simple rule that multiplying the middle number of an odd-sided magic square by the number of rows in the square gives the magic constant.

## Beating the logic puzzles

Learning a little bit of math means that you will be able to recognize the patterns used in logic puzzles such as these, which should help you work out how to solve them. Some scientific studies have shown that exercising your brain regularly with logic problems like this can help keep your mind in better shape as you grow older.

# How to make sure you pay off your credit card

Have you ever wondered why credit card companies set their minimum repayment at the level they do? What you may not realize is that a small change in the amount of your monthly repayment can translate into a huge difference in the amount of time it takes to pay the balance off, since the accrued interest is so much higher—something the credit card companies know very well.

## Compound interest

A few years ago, it was virtually standard that the minimum monthly repayment for a credit card was 5 percent of the remaining balance. These days, you can find credit companies who let you pay off a minimum of just 2.5 percent of the balance. Credit card companies (as well as banks, mortgage lenders, and loan providers) use something called the compound interest equation to calculate how much your repayments should be.

As well as showing that if you do not pay off more than the

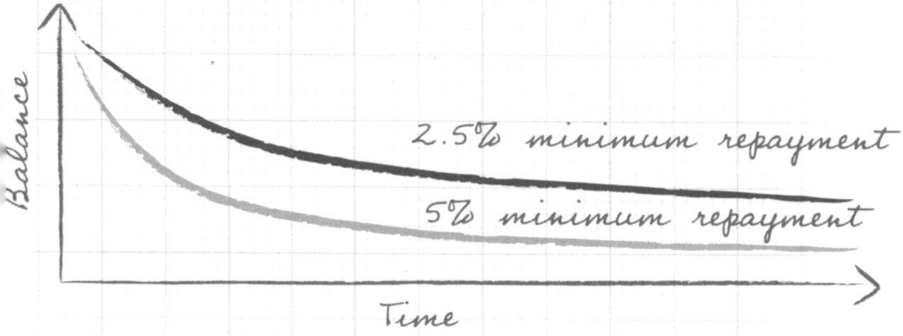

Fig. 1 Compound interest graph

minimum repayment each month, you will never pay off your debt, the graph (Fig. 1) on the previous page also shows the impact of different levels of minimum repayment. Notice how much more slowly your balance falls if you only pay a minimum of 2.5 percent instead of 5 percent.

The equations show that doubling your monthly repayment from 2.5 to 5 percent more than halves the amount of time it will take to pay off your debt and drastically cuts the total amount of interest you pay. That's why paying more than the minimum monthly repayment makes such good financial sense. The scary truth about the compound interest equation is that if you always pay your minimum payment and no more, you will never pay off your balance. (In fact, credit card companies have a fixed monthly repayment of, say, $15 so that you do end up paying it off at some point.) Invest in a bit of math and you'll be reaping dividends.

## Paying the balance

Imagine you have a credit card which charges 12 percent interest a year (compounded on a monthly basis), an outstanding balance (which we will call $B_0$) and a minimum monthly payment of 5 percent of the outstanding balance.

After each month, your new outstanding balance is the balance from the previous month plus the interest on that balance, less the minimum repayment. So after one month your new balance (which we will call $B_1$) is as follows:

$$B_1 = B_0 + (B_0 \times 1\%) - (B_0 \times 5\%) = B_0 \times 96\%$$

If your original balance was \$1,000 (and you don't spend any more during the month on the card) then after one month, the balance is \$1,000 + \$10 –\$50, or \$960.

After the second month, the balance (which we call $B_2$) is given by:

$$B_2 = B_1 + (B_1 \times 1\%) - (B_1 \times 5\%) = B_1 \times 96\%$$

which looks very similar to the equation for the first month.

In fact, since we know that $B_1 = B_0 \times 96\%$, we can now write:

$$B_2 = B_0 \times 96\% \times 96\%$$

It is easy to show that the balance remaining after $n$ months is given by the original balance multiplied by 96 percent $n$ times, which mathematicians write as follows:

$$B_n = B_0 \times (96\%)n$$

Let's imagine some future time when you have paid off your balance, i.e., $B_n$ falls to zero. It should be obvious with a bit of playing on a calculator that no matter how big you make the number $n$ in the above, $B_n$ never quite reaches zero. So looking at these equations for compound interest we can see that by making minimum repayments only, even without additional spending, you will never be able to clear your balance.

# How to use vinegar as a cleaning product

Open the cupboard underneath the sink in almost any house and you are likely to be faced with a plethora of cleaning chemicals—glass and mirror sprays, floor cleaners, furniture polish. But before all these modern cleaners came along, a popular cleaning agent was simple white vinegar, thanks to its versatility, and science shows that it really can work.

Vinegar is a dilute solution of ethanoic acid (also known as acetic acid), which has the chemical formula $CH_3COOH$. Like other acids, acetic acid neutralizes chemicals called bases or alkalis to produce mineral salts and water, and reactions such as these make it an effective cleaning product.

## Hard water stains

White vinegar is an effective hard water stain remover. This white, chalky deposit that gathers around kettles, heating elements, and toilets is usually made of a substance called calcium carbonate, which has the chemical formula $CaCO_3$.

When acetic acid comes into contact with calcium carbonate, the following chemical reaction occurs:

$$2CH_3COOH + CaCO_3 \longrightarrow (CH_3COO)_2Ca + CO_2 + H_2O$$

The last two items on the right should be recognizable as carbon dioxide and water. The other is known as calcium acetate or calcium ethanoate (the calcium salt of acetic acid).

## Soap scum

Vinegar can also be used to remove soap scum and is useful for unblocking drains when combined with baking soda.

Baking soda has the chemical formula $NaHCO_3$, and this reacts with acetic acid according to the following reaction:

$$CH_3COOH + NaHCO_3 \longrightarrow CH_3COONa + H_2CO_3$$

The two compounds on the right-hand side of this equation are sodium acetate, a type of salt, and carbonic acid. The carbonic acid quickly decomposes into water and carbon dioxide. The carbon dioxide creates foaming and bubbling, and helps dislodge the material blocking the drain.

## Tarnished copper

Vinegar can also be used to clean tarnished copper (copper oxide, $CuO$), including copper coins. A solution of vinegar and table salt ($NaCl$) will rapidly remove the tarnish. The reaction is as follows:

$$CuO + 2CH_3COOH \longrightarrow Cu(CH_3COO)_2 + H_2O$$

$Cu(CH_3COO)_2$ is a salt known as copper acetate, which is soluble in water. The table salt acts as a catalyst, making the reaction proceed much more quickly than it otherwise would.

## Bacteria

There have also been many claims regarding vinegar's use to combat bacteria on surfaces around the home. A study by William A. Rutala and colleagues at the University of North Carolina in 2000 tested vinegar and baking soda against a range of microbes. The scientists found that vinegar did substantially reduce the levels of the microbes *Pseudomonas aeruginosa* and *Salmonella choleraesuis*. However, its effect on levels of *Escherichia coli* and *Staphylococcus aureus* was not very impressive compared to using household cleaning chemicals.

# How to remove red wine stains

Throwing a party at home seems like a great idea until someone spills the first glass of red wine on the deep pile carpet. Yet the application of science—and chemistry in particular—can help you relax in the event of a spill.

When the inevitable glass of wine is knocked over at a party, there is usually no shortage of people to rush up with suggestions on how best to deal with it. Some will suggest throwing on white wine, others insist on club soda being the best remedy, another faction will get ready with handfuls of salt, while yet another group will race off to the kitchen to find paper towels and water.

If you have the misfortune to spill a red wine that has aged for a few years, it is even more of a nightmare. Not only are you out the cost of what was probably an expensive bottle of wine, but getting the stain out is ever harder. Stains that have been left to dry overnight are also harder to remove. What action should you really take against the stain? Science is here to help.

# Why does red wine stain?

Red wine comes in many shades—from dark pink to ruby red to purply-black. This spectrum of colors is due to a group of chemicals called anthocyanins, which give the color to all sorts of fruit and vegetables, including cherries, red cabbage, aubergines, and the "red" grapes that give red wine its color. There are hundreds of different anthocyanins, but they all have a very similar chemical structure that allows the pigment to easily attach itself to materials such as carpet fibers.

In aged red wine, the chemistry becomes more complex. In these, anthocyanins combine with the tannins in the wine to make more complex molecules that are even tougher to remove.

So what about all the traditional remedies that people recommend for red wine stains? Are they based on any scientific evidence at all, and do they actually work?

## Salt

Salt, or sodium chloride, is unreactive when it comes to anthocyanins, so the chemistry says that it should not be particularly effective. But although the salt is no good for removing the pigment, it does have another useful property—it is very good at absorbing liquids, and this is the scientific basis for using it to remove red wine. Rather than treating the stain itself, all you are doing is absorbing the liquid. Naturally, salt will not work on dried stains.

## Club soda

Club soda is made up of water, some bubbles of carbon dioxide, and trace amounts of mineral salts, such as sodium bicarbonate or potassium sulfate. As explained above, salts have little chemical effect on anthocyanins, but with club soda it's actually the bubbles that can have an effect. An increasing number of cleaning compounds foam or bubble with carbon dioxide to help with their cleaning action. There is some evidence that bubbles of carbon dioxide help in lifting stains from materials, yet the effect is minimal and the addition of carbon dioxide–producing chemicals is more about the theatricality of a foaming cleaning material rather than its efficacy.

## White wine

The major difference between red wine and white wine is the method of production. The former are usually made using the pulp of grapes along with grape skins; white wine is usually made without the skins. Since it is the grape skin that contains most of the anthocyanins, this tells us why white wine does not leave stains as badly as red wine. When it comes to using it to combat red wine, since white wine has identical constituents, there is no wonder ingredient that causes it to erase the red wine stain magically.

## Water

Because of anthocyanins' dark pigment, many people look to using fruits and vegetables high in natural anthocyanins as natural alternatives to chemical dyes. However, anthocyanins have one very major disadvantage: they are water soluble, due to the presence of sugar in the complex molecule. If you try to dye a fabric with something like mashed-up red cabbage, the purple color in your clothes will soon wash out.

The water solubility of anthocyanins is their weak point. It turns out that adding water to most anthocyanins converts them to another form of anthocyanin but, and this is crucial, a colorless form of anthocyanin.

In fact, this is the key factor in most of the proposed methods for removing stains—they contain water. What this means is that the most effective way to get rid of red wine stains (without resorting to strong chemicals) is to use water, and plenty of it. As soon as the wine is spilled, pour plenty of water on to it.

If you don't have water, then white wine and club soda are good alternatives, but mainly because they dilute the red wine in the stain.

## Blotting

You should always avoid rubbing. This is because you risk working the wine deeper into the fabric. Instead, take a clean cloth or some paper towels and blot up the copious amounts of water/wine mixture that is on the fabric.

## The scientific method

Proper scientific research has been carried out on various types of stain removers by Dr. Andrew Waterhouse, a professor of oenology at the University of California, Davis. He tested various methods, including white wine, salt, and chemical cleaners that you can buy over the counter.

The trial looked at the efficacy of the various methods on silk, cotton, polyester-cotton blend, and nylon. The remedies were applied two minutes after the spill and a second time a day later, and then left to stand for three hours. After that they were washed in cold water and dried.

The research found that the most effective stain remover was a concoction of hydrogen peroxide and liquid soap, although no remedy was particularly effective for the more delicate fabrics such as silk.

Some commercial cleaning products include a chemical called sodium percarbonate, and this combines the effect of hydrogen peroxide with an unusual property of anthocyanins.

Anthocyanins act a little like the litmus paper you used in chemistry class in that they change color between blue and red according to whether the solution they are exposed to is acidic or alkaline. Sodium percarbonate is alkaline and turns anthocyanins blue, before they are bleached by the hydrogen peroxide, giving your fabric that infamous bluish whiteness that cleaning product companies like to talk about.

So next time someone knocks over a glass of red wine, you now know exactly what to do about it, and which myths to lay to rest.

# How to win at Scrabble

It's happened again. Despite a solid performance involving what you thought were brilliantly ingenious words, you've been beaten by your know-it-all grandmother. How does she do it every time? Scrabble isn't just about making the longest words possible from the available letters (unless you're using all seven). There are techniques you can use based on the distribution of the letters and their scores.

## Frequencies and scores

The English version of Scrabble contains 100 tiles, with the values and frequencies shown in the table below, plus two blank tiles.

| Letter | Value | Number of tiles in game | Letter | Value | Number of tiles in game |
|--------|-------|-------------------------|--------|-------|-------------------------|
| A | 1 | 9 | N | 1 | 6 |
| B | 3 | 2 | O | 1 | 8 |
| C | 3 | 2 | P | 3 | 2 |
| D | 2 | 4 | Q | 10 | 1 |
| E | 1 | 12 | R | 1 | 6 |
| F | 4 | 2 | S | 1 | 4 |
| G | 2 | 3 | T | 1 | 6 |
| H | 4 | 2 | U | 1 | 4 |
| I | 1 | 9 | V | 4 | 2 |
| J | 8 | 1 | W | 4 | 2 |
| K | 5 | 1 | X | 8 | 1 |
| L | 1 | 4 | Y | 4 | 2 |
| M | 3 | 2 | Z | 10 | 1 |

## Letter distributions

The distribution of letters has remained unchanged since the game was invented by Alfred Butts.

So how did Butts come up with this distribution? He did so by analyzing the frequency that letters appeared on the front page of the *New York Times*. This, he felt, was a good sample of the English language.

In fact, a science called frequency analysis shows that the approximate frequency of the various letters in English is as shown in the following bar chart (Fig. 1).

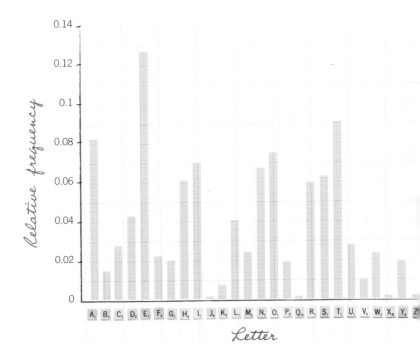

*Fig. 1 A frequency analysis chart*

You can see that E is the most common letter, and this is reflected by the large number of tiles in Scrabble and the letter's low value. You can also see how Q and Z are the least common, which is why they are worth ten points.

The bar chart also shows some anomalies. You can see that H is a particularly valuable letter to have in your rack—it occurs almost as often as I, O, and N yet is worth four times as many points.

## Thinking ahead

Knowing the distributions of the letters is essential for any good Scrabble player. Imagine, for example, you have picked up the following: AAFEERM. The temptation might be to take the consonants F, R, and M and place them around an O on the board to make FROM or FORM. However, given that vowels are by far the most common letters, you could risk ending up with something like AAEEIIO—much harder to use effectively.

## Stem words

One of the key strategies is to aim for bingos, the 50-point bonuses you get for using all seven letters. Many top Scrabble players learn six-letter stem words that can be used to create large numbers of possible seven-letter bingo words. So knowing what letters are most likely to come up can help you to decide which letters to keep for next time to make up a stem. The best stem to aim for is SATINE (itself a word) as it can be used to create seven-letter bingo words with every single letter of the alphabet other than J. For example, if you have SATINE and pick up a U, you can make AUNTIES. Pick up a G and you have SEATING. Pick up a D and you have INSTEAD. Many of the words created this way are quite obscure, so make sure you have a big vocabulary or a good dictionary by your side.

# How to chill a bottle of wine quickly

Whether you're an amateur sommelier and want to serve your wine at the exact recommended temperature, or the particular bottle you want has been kept in a cupboard instead of the fridge, sometimes you need to be able to chill a bottle of wine in a hurry.

## What temperature should wine be served at?

First, what temperature should the wine be? Many people swear by serving red wine at room temperature. However, these days most houses are centrally heated and typically have a temperature between 68° and 77°F (20° and 25°C). In fact, most red wines taste best between 57° and 64°F (14° and 18°C), so if the bottle has been sitting in a wine rack in your kitchen, it is best to chill it slightly.

We also have a tendency to serve bottles of white wine straight from the fridge. A typical fridge maintains a temperature between 32° and 41°F (0° and 5°C). However, most whites are better drunk slightly warmer than this, around 45° or 46°F (7° or 8°C).

Some wines do not fit these general temperature recommendations. Beaujolais and full-bodied white wines such as white Burgundies are better served at around 50°F (10°C).

So now that we know what sort of temperatures are best for drinking wine, how do we achieve them?

## Warming up

Since most of us do not have the luxury of a wine cellar that keeps wines (white ones at least) at around the temperature we want to drink them, many of us use the fridge. You should take a white wine out of the fridge before you serve it so that it warms up a few degrees to the optimum temperature. Exactly how long will depend on the temperature of your house, but 10 or 15 minutes should make it taste that little bit better if you can resist the temptation for that long. For red wines stored at room temperature, the problem is the opposite, and you should either put the wine in the fridge for a few minutes or cool it down a little in an ice bucket before serving.

## The chill factor

For most of us the problem is getting a bottle of wine chilled in a hurry. Using the fridge is the slowest option, as it will take a couple of hours to chill something down from room temperature. So if you need to chill a bottle of wine fast, there are a number of other options: the freezer, a wine sleeve, or an ice bucket.

Many people argue that you should never chill a wine in the freezer, but that is not true. If you chill your bottle of white down to the optimum 45° or 46°F (7° or 8°C), then a freezer is just fine. It will take approximately half an hour. If you leave your wine in longer than that, that's when problems occur. Wine freezes at a higher temperature than water because of the alcohol content. As it cools down toward this temperature, crystals start to form in the wine that can affect its flavor. If you leave it even longer, you might end up with a broken bottle and wine all over your freezer. There are a number of wine sleeves on the market that contain a special gel. Put them in the freezer and then take them out when needed—just slip them over your warm bottle. It works faster than using the freezer directly because the wine is chilled by direct conduction of heat rather than by convection through the air.

Ice buckets are the time-honored method of chilling wine, but science has something to say here too. A bucket containing ice on its own is not as effective as a bucket containing a mix of ice and cold water. The latter will chill your wine to drinking temperature in around twenty minutes. You can speed this up even further. We all know that road crews spread salt on icy roads to melt the ice. This is because salt lowers the freezing point of water. Adding salt to your ice bucket has the same effect, allowing it to absorb more heat from your bottle of wine before melting (see Fig. 1).

Add salt

ice

Fig. 1
Chilling
wine using
salt and ice

# How to save gas

With fuel being so expensive, it is inevitable that motorists might think about driving less to cut down on their costs, but for many people that's just not an option. However, by being aware of some of the science behind our fuel consumption there are other ways we can cut down on our costs, by changing the way we drive.

In the past few years the price of oil has reached atmospheric heights. In July 2008, the price of a barrel of crude oil nearly reached $150. That compares to an average of just $26.64 per barrel for the whole of the period from 1945 to 2008. As a result, the cost of gasoline and petrol rose sharply. In that same month, the price of a gallon of regular gas in the US averaged a record $4.11, while in the UK petrol cost just a shade under £1.20 for a liter (£6 a gallon) in the same month, a figure which was eclipsed in April 2010.

## The equation of motion

In order to know how to change our driving habits, we need to understand a little bit about the science and the equations involved in the acceleration of a car and the forces that act against it.

Newton's equation of motion, $F=ma$, is probably one of the best-known equations in science. It tells us how much force, $F$, is required to accelerate an object of mass $m$ with acceleration $a$. This can clearly be applied to an accelerating car.

Yet this does not give the whole picture. We need to consider other forces acting on the car, and there are a number of forces at play, such as the amount of drag, the friction of the tires on the road surface, and the internal friction in the engine. Each of them has an effect on the amount of fuel you require.

## The drag equation

One of the limiting factors on how fast a car travels is the drag on the car caused by the resistance of the air through which it travels. This force acts in the opposite direction to that of the driving force, which is accelerating the car.

Physicists show this effect through something called the drag equation, as follows:

$$F_D = \tfrac{1}{2}\rho v^2 C_d A$$

where $F_D$ is the force on the car due to drag, $\rho$ is the density of air (a constant), $v$ is the velocity of the car, $C_d$ is the drag coefficient (see below) and $A$ is the cross-sectional area of the car presented to the direction of travel.

## Low drag coefficients

The drag coefficient is what car (and aircraft) designers aim to reduce when they are designing new models—an object with lower drag coefficient is less affected by drag than one with a higher drag coefficient (see Fig. 1 and Fig. 2). Here are some typical values of $C_d$ for a range of objects.

The cross-sectional area also plays a part, as you can see from the equation above. Designers try to minimize the value of $C_d$ multiplied by $A$

| Object | $C_d$ |
|---|---|
| Boeing 787 | 0.024 |
| Toyota Prius | 0.25 |
| Mini Cooper | 0.35 |
| Ford Mustang | 0.46 |
| Citroën 2CV | 0.51 |
| Hummer H2 | 0.57 |
| Upright person | 1 |
| Brick | 2.1 |

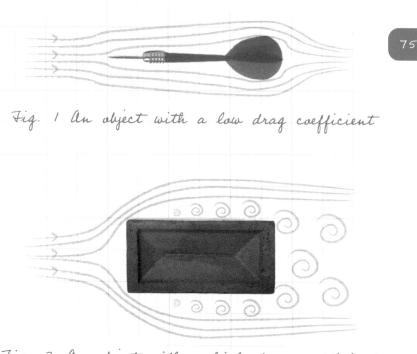

Fig. 1 An object with a low drag coefficient

Fig. 2 An object with a high drag coefficient

for a particular car. So just having a car with a low $C_dA$ reduces drag and can help us save fuel.

Of course, you don't necessarily want to go out and buy a new car with a lower $C_dA$, but there are a number of other factors related to these equations that will also reduce your fuel consumption and that you can change.

## Reducing the weight

Another equation mentioned in the same breath as Newton's $F=ma$ is $W=Fd$ or, in plain English, work equals force times distance. This equation can tell us how much work (energy) is expended by a force over a given distance $d$. We can combine the two to give:

$$W = mad$$

What this equation tells us is that if the acceleration and the distance are fixed, then the amount of work done depends on the mass—i.e., a lower-mass car uses less energy to accelerate over a fixed distance.

Therefore, reducing the mass of your car helps. Of course, we can't reduce the mass of the actual car, but we can reduce the mass of things inside the car. Carrying lots of heavy things in your trunk is a sure way to waste fuel.

## Smooth acceleration

The equation also tells us something else. For a fixed mass and distance, the work done (energy expended) is proportional to the acceleration. Accelerating quickly uses more energy than accelerating smoothly. This is why driving smoothly rather than in bursts of high speed and rapid deceleration uses less fuel.

## Streamlining your vehicle

In the drag equation, we already saw that a low $C_dA$ translates into lower drag from air resistance. This should tell us that driving with a roof rack on top of the car or with the sunroof open when you don't need to is bad for fuel efficiency.

## Slow but steady

We can also use the drag equation to work out how much power we need to overcome drag. This is given by:

$$P_d = F_dv = \tfrac{1}{2}\rho v^3$$

Since for a given car $C_dA$ is a constant and the density of air is a constant, the only factor that is variable on the right-hand side is the velocity. We should note that it is not just the velocity on the right but the cube of the velocity. In practice this means that if you double your speed, the power needed to overcome the air drag multiplies eightfold (since $2^3 = 8$). This shows us that driving more slowly is more fuel efficient.

## Tires and friction

The effect of friction from the road cannot be ignored either. Car manufacturers give recommended tire pressures because correctly inflated tires have less friction than underinflated tires. The classic flat-bottomed underinflated tire has more rubber in contact with the road surface. So make sure you keep your tires properly inflated to reduce the friction.

## Economic gear shifts

Finally, you should consider the speed that your engine is turning over. As we said above, internal friction in the engine plays a part in fuel efficiency. The higher the rpm, the greater the internal friction. This is why you should shift gears as soon as is practical. Most experts recommend that you shift gears before you reach 2,500 rpm in a gas engine and 2,000 rpm in a diesel engine.

Aesop's fable *The Hare and the Tortoise* told us that slow and steady wins the race. It turns out that it also helps us save fuel.

# How to save water

Water is the new oil, they tell us. What they mean is that in an increasingly thirsty world, a growing population with a raging appetite for water-intensive crops and industries will go to extreme lengths to get their hands on fresh water.

Whether you want to help the environment, save water during a dry spell, or just save some money on your water bills, there are plenty of different reasons for saving water, and plenty of ways to do it. Here we will look at saving water in one of the most frequently used, and most wasteful, household appliances: the flush toilet. We can save water using a principle of water displacement supposedly discovered by the Greek mathematician and physicist Archimedes.

## A eureka moment

If you have ever had a eureka moment—the time when suddenly everything becomes clear about a problem that has been bugging you—then you are paying tribute to Archimedes.

The most famous story about him comes to us today through the writings of the architect Marcus Vitruvius Pollio. He tells the story of how one King Hiero had been given a golden crown. At the time, there were rumors that the crown had been made from a mixture of gold and silver by some unscrupulous goldsmith, and Hiero wanted to find out if the rumors were true. The crown could have been melted down to see if it had the same density as gold but that would have destroyed it.

Archimedes, lying in his bath, had a brainstorm. He noticed that as his body became immersed, the water ran out of the vessel. He realized that a similar method could be applied to the crown;

gold and silver have different densities, which means that a lump of gold will weigh about twice that of a lump of silver of the same size. Therefore, he could compare the crown to a block of gold of the same weight by immersing them in water and comparing the amount of water that ran out. If the crown was not made of pure gold, it would have to be bulkier to make up the weight.

Vitruvius reports that when Archimedes realized he had solved the problem, he leapt out of the bath in joy, and ran through the streets naked, crying out *"Eureka!"* ("I have found it out.") Using the technique, he found that the crown had indeed been made using a mix of gold and silver, thus exposing the corrupt goldsmith.

## Water wasting appliances

In Great Britain, the average household water consumption in houses without a water meter was 40 gallons (150 liters) per person per day in 2008–09. In the US, average water consumption is two to three times that. That is an awful lot of water.

For most households, flushing the toilet is the most water-guzzling activity there is, particularly if you live in a house with an older toilet. These can use up to 4½ gallons (17 liters) with every flush. Newer toilets use half that. When you think that people use the toilet on average five times a day, you can see how our daily water consumption is so high.

## Reducing water waste

So how can we use Archimedes' principle in practice to save water? The answer lies in your toilet tank. Older toilet models use so much more water because the tank is designed to hold much more water than the newer models. That quantity of water generally isn't needed to flush a toilet. The Archimedes principle tells us that putting an object in your tank—a brick or a filled water bottle are the classic objects—will displace an amount of water equal to its own volume (see Fig. 1). That means that every time you flush your toilet and the tank refills, it uses one brick's worth less of water.

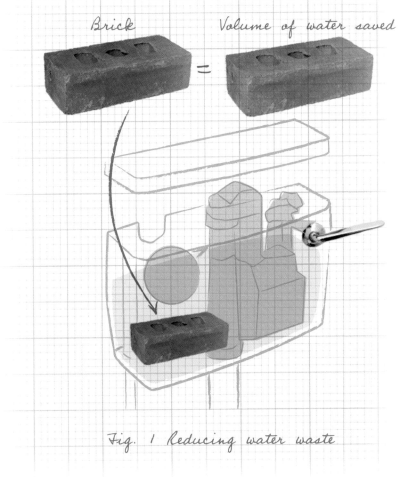

Brick    Volume of water saved

Fig. 1 Reducing water waste

# How to build a fire

If you have ever tried to light a fire, whether it is a coal or log fire in the home, or a charcoal barbecue or a bonfire in the backyard, you will know that getting it to stay lit can be a real challenge. You cannot simply light a match and apply it to the coal or wood. It may start burning, but it will usually splutter out after a few minutes. To build a fire that stays lit requires the application of a bit of science.

## The chemical reaction

What, exactly, is a fire? Many people are surprised to learn that a fire is actually a manifestation of a *chemical* rather than a *physical* process. The combustion of a fuel is given by the typical reaction:

$$\text{Fuel + Oxygen} \longrightarrow \text{Carbon dioxide + water + heat}$$

However, this is the perfect scenario when all of the fuel achieves combustion. In reality, the reaction is not complete and you are left with other by-products of combustion, such as carbon monoxide and ash or soot (carbon).

The reaction above is usually written by chemists as:

$$C_xH_y + (x + \tfrac{y}{4})O_2 \longrightarrow xCO_2 + (\tfrac{y}{2})H_2O$$

where the $C_xH_y$ represents a hydrocarbon fuel of some kind. For example, butane, the gas that is often used in camping stoves, has the formula $C_4H_{10}$ and burns according to the chemical reaction below:

$$2C_4H_{10} + 13O_2 \longrightarrow 8CO_2 + 10H_2O$$

This sort of chemical reaction is called exothermic, meaning that it produces heat or light—in this case, in the form of a flame or the glow of embers.

Coal and wood are complex materials made up of lots of different organic (carbon-containing) materials, but the combustion of each of these occurs in a similar way.

In fact, the equation does not tell the whole story. Why does the simple act of exposing a fuel to the air cause it to burst into flames? In reality, the equation should look more like this:

$$\text{Heat + fuel + oxygen} \longrightarrow \text{Carbon dioxide + water + more heat}$$

You need some initial heat to get the process of combustion started, and the reaction itself produces more heat creating a chain reaction until the fuel is exhausted. This is why we use matches to start a fire.

## Building your fire

So now we know the science behind fire, how does this help us to build a fire that will stay lit? The equations serve to help us understand what makes a fire burn and, therefore, what we can do to improve the conditions so the fire stays lit. In the first part of the word equation above, we can see the most important ingredients for a fire—an initial form of heat, some fuel and some oxygen. To keep the fire going we need to make sure the initial heat is there for long enough, and that there is sufficient oxygen and fuel, to sustain a chain reaction.

## Sustaining the heat

A match will quickly go out, so we need to find a way to keep the initial heat sustained. This is why we often use tinder, some easily combustible material such as dry leaves or a rolled-up newspaper to sustain the initial flame.

## Surface area

The next thing we need to do is make sure there is enough oxygen. This sounds odd—surely the amount of oxygen in the air is fixed? What's important is how much oxygen is in contact with the surface of the material being burned.

Imagine you had a cube of wood measuring 10 inches on each edge. Each face has a surface area of 100 square inches and there are six faces. The cube has a surface area of 600 square inches.

Now cut the cube into eight smaller cubes of 5 inches on each edge. Each face of the smaller cube has a surface area of 5 x 5 = 25 square inches and each cube therefore has a surface area of 6 x 25 = 150 square inches. Those eight smaller cubes now have a combined surface area of 8 x 150 = 1,200 square inches. This means that for the same volume of initial material we have doubled the surface area.

If we now see how those cubes burn, we will discover that the smaller cubes burn more easily because of their larger surface area in contact with the air. This is the basis of kindling. Kindling refers to material such as dry twigs or smaller batons of wood chopped up from a larger log. In the latter case, a bundle of kindling will have a higher surface-to-volume ratio than the corresponding log from which it was chopped.

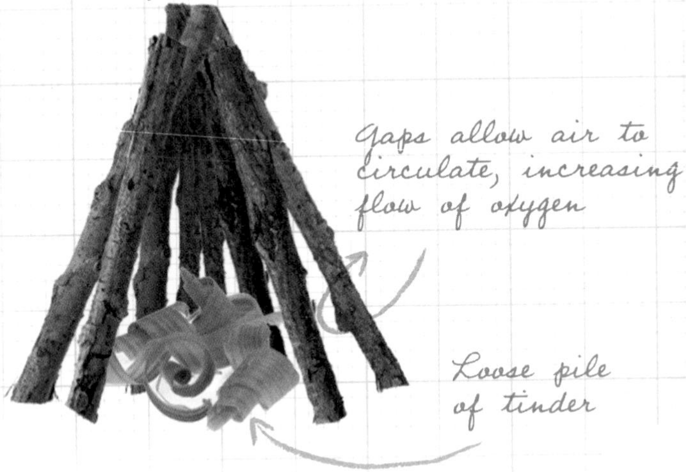

Fig. 1 The tepee method

Gaps allow air to circulate, increasing flow of oxygen

Loose pile of tinder

## Tepee fire

You can probably conclude from this discussion that stacking the bundle of kindling closely together is not a good idea—you are reducing the surface area by doing so. This is why many people use the tepee method of building a fire. In this, you place your tinder in a loose pile at the center of where you want the fire. You then build a tepee-shaped pile of kindling above it. This allows air to circulate freely around the kindling and also keeps the supply of fuel in the right place—as the tinder catches fire the kindling is well placed above it to start burning and then fall into the tinder to keep it going (see Fig. 1).

## Charcoal pyramid

A similar method can be used to light a charcoal barbecue without resorting to dangerous ideas such as adding lighter fluid. Simply build a loose pyramid of charcoal lumps above your tinder material. The gaps between the lumps will be enough to keep it going. Once the charcoal has caught fire, spread it over the base of the barbecue.

## Log cabin

Another popular method for a wood fire is to build a miniature log cabin from sticks. Place two sticks of kindling parallel to each other on either side of the tinder. Now place two more at right angles to these to form a square and continue building up the layers of your "cabin." Don't forget to add a roof above the tinder once it is lit. The gaps between the miniature logs will be enough to keep the fire lit (see Fig. 2).

Once the kindling is lit, it is then a matter of placing your main fuel around it to keep the fire going. Bear in mind the necessity of keeping the oxygen flowing. You shouldn't pack the main material too tightly together, and you can also increase the flow of oxygen by fanning the flames.

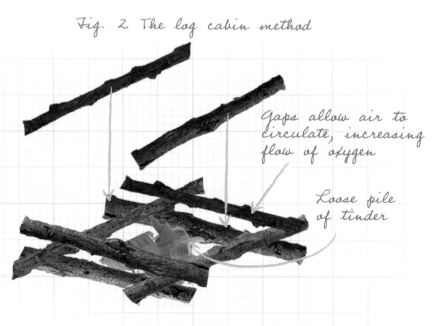

Fig. 2 The log cabin method

Gaps allow air to circulate, increasing flow of oxygen

Loose pile of tinder

# How to deice your car quickly

It's a ritual that can add a good 15 minutes to your commute during winter—removing the ice from the car windows so you can see clearly enough to drive safely. Everyone has their own favored method for getting rid of ice, but what is the best method according to science? Understanding what causes frost and ice to form on cars is the first step.

## Morning frost

Water vapor is in the air all around us, but it is usually only visible when it is foggy, or in the morning as dew or frost. Warm air is able to hold (or more accurately, exist side by side with) more water vapor than cold air. As the temperature decreases, you eventually reach a point known as the dewpoint, the temperature at which the air is completely saturated with water vapor and can no longer hold any more. At this point the water starts to turn into its liquid form, known as condensation. It is this water that appears as fog, dew, and, if the surface temperature is colder than freezing, ice.

Large expanses of metal and glass are able to radiate heat faster than things like pavement or lawn and are colder as a result, so sometimes you might find that the windows of your car are frosted over even when there isn't any frost on the ground.

## Prevention is the best cure

Now we know what has caused the ice to form, what can we do about it? In fact, the best and most convenient strategy is to avoid the problem altogether by reducing the chances of ice forming in the first place.

Perhaps the easiest method of all is to cover your windshield overnight with a light tarpaulin. The air gap between the tarp and the windshield acts as an insulator and stops the windshield from icing over, although the tarp itself will get icy. However, the tarpaulin can be removed quite easily.

An alternative prevention method is to apply a deicer beforehand to keep ice from forming. A simple solution of three parts white vinegar to one part water placed into a spray gun can be used as a very effective ice-prevention spray. The main chemical constituent of vinegar is ethanoic (or acetic) acid. On its own, this acid freezes at 62.4°F (16.9°C)—i.e., above freezing and just below room temperature. However, if it is diluted, then the freezing point of the solution is lower than the freezing point of water, which is what makes it effective in preventing ice.

A solution containing 70 percent medical rubbing alcohol (which has ethanol) and dishwashing liquid also works well as a deicer. If you know it is going to be a cold night, spray all of the windows with your homemade concoction after you have parked your car.

Deicing mix:

1 part water

3 parts vinegar

Of course, knowing how to prevent it isn't very helpful if it's already the morning, you didn't know it was going to be so cold overnight, and you are now confronted with ice on your windows. There are a number of different ways that you can try to tackle the ice.

## Heat

The most obvious idea is to raise the temperature of the windshield. Using the car's heater might seem like the best choice, but this is probably the most time consuming. The air is generally directed into small patches and it can take many minutes to clear the windshield to the point where it is safe and legal to drive.

## Boiling water

Another method some people use is to pour boiling water over the windshield. This is not a good idea in general. Things expand when they are heated up and glass is no exception. However, if you pour a pot of hot water over your windshield, initially it will just heat up and expand in the places where the water runs. The uneven expansion sets up stresses in the glass and can cause it to shatter. Windshields are designed to be strong, but if you have chips or cracks in the glass caused by stones, these can weaken it.

If you do use water, use cold water first and then tepid water to clear the windshield. However, if it is really cold, adding cold water might actually make the problem worse since the water will just freeze on contact.

## Deicing sprays

Car deicing sprays are also popular. These typically contain some form of alcohol, such as methanol or isopropyl alcohol. The science behind these is that the freezing point of alcohol is far lower than that of water. The most effective ones contain methanol, which freezes at $-143°F$ ($-97°C$) as opposed to $32°F$ ($0°C$) for water. As the deicer liquid mixes with any liquid water on the windshield, it causes the neighboring ice to melt.

## Brute force

Physical methods, such as using an ice scraper or a credit card, can work with a thin coating of ice, but thicker sheets of ice can take longer. However, scraping methods—particularly if you use something other than a proper scraper—can result in minute scratches on the windshield that affect visibility.

In fact, the most effective approach to deicing your car, if you weren't prepared for an icy morning, is a combination of these methods; put your heater on for a bit of extra heat, spray on a deicer that contains methanol, and resort to a scraper for any stubborn areas that refuse to melt.

# How to make your cakes and bread rise

Home baking can be great fun, bringing together some basic ingredients, mixing them up and then watching them turn into a piping hot loaf of bread, a delicious cake, or a fluffy soufflé in the oven. But many times when we open the oven door, our excitement turns to disappointment, as our creation collapses before our very eyes. What went wrong?

## Baking powder

It is carbon dioxide that makes cakes rise, so the mixture needs plenty of it. The key ingredient to ensure this when making cakes, muffins, and scones is baking powder. (Note that self-rising flour already has this mixed into it.) This is a white powder typically made up of an alkali (a type of mineral salt made from a metal such as sodium), an acidic salt, and some starch. Normally, acids and alkalis neutralize each other. But the starch keeps them from reacting prematurely, and they will only do so in the presence of water, heat, or both.

In most cases, the alkali salt in baking powder is sodium bicarbonate (also known as baking soda), which has the chemical formula $NaHCO_3$. The generalized chemical reaction that drives the rising process is:

$$NaHCO_3 + H^+ \longrightarrow Na^+ + CO_2 + H_2O$$

$H^+$ is ionized hydrogen (a hydrogen atom with its electron stripped off) and occurs in the food as a result of the acid in the baking powder. The right-hand side of the equation shows the carbon dioxide that causes the cake to rise.

Frequently, the acidic salt in baking powder is cream of tartar (potassium hydrogen tartrate), which has the chemical symbol $KHC_4H_4O_6$. In that case, the reaction proceeds as follows:

$$NaHCO_3 + KHC_4H_4O_6 \longrightarrow KNaC_4H_4O_6 + CO_2 + H_2O$$

## Collapsing quick fix

If your cakes, muffins, and scones aren't rising, there could be a couple of reasons. The first answer could be excess acid. As we saw above, the carbon dioxide is created from the reaction between the alkaline and the acidic elements of the baking powder. For best results, the amounts of acid and alkali need to be neatly balanced. This is why recipes are so prescriptive about the amounts of each ingredient required. Stick to the recipe as much as possible.

But even if you do follow the recipes to the letter, there are other factors involved in the failure of cakes, bread, and soufflés to rise, including the atmospheric pressure. On a day when a low pressure system is hanging over your region, your cake will rise more than on a high pressure day. The difference may be so much that the structure becomes unstable. Cutting back on the baking powder in your cake by a small amount (perhaps a quarter of a teaspoon for every teaspoon in the recipe) can help overcome it.

## Bread bubbles

Things are slightly different for bread. The relevant ingredient in bread is yeast. Yeast, as most people probably don't want to be reminded, is a micro-organism belonging to the fungi family, just like mushrooms. The species *Saccharomyces cerevisiae* is the one most commonly used as baker's yeast.

Yeast thrives by eating carbohydrates such as starch and sugar, breaking them down into less complex molecules and releasing carbon dioxide in the process. In bread, the yeast consumes the starch present in the flour. The carbon dioxide that results is what makes the bread rise (see Fig. 1). There is also another surprising by-product: ethyl alcohol. Yet bread is not likely to make you drunk—the alcohol evaporates off when the dough is cooked, unlike in the brewer's fermentation process, which also works on the same principle.

The carbon dioxide generated by yeast bubbling away through the dough does not evaporate, of course. Wheat flour contains two proteins called glutenin and gliadin which, when combined with water, form gluten. Gluten gives bread dough its stretchy

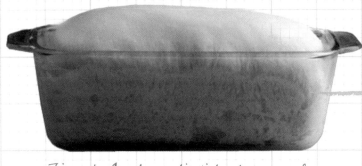

Fig. 1 Carbon dioxide forms when the dough is left to rest

stickiness. When you knead dough, it creates a microscopic network of criss-crossing strands of gluten. The carbon dioxide gets caught in this sticky blanket, causing the dough to rise and the loaf of bread to gain volume (see Fig. 2).

Bread problems often occur because you have allowed the dough to rise too much in the first place. The carbon dioxide bubbles can become too large and just collapse when the bread is baked. So for a perfect loaf, follow the recipe instructions to the letter for how long to let your dough rise.

## Soufflé structure

What about soufflés? Soufflés rise not because of carbon dioxide but because of trapped air, and we have to introduce this into the mixture mechanically rather than chemically. This is what whisking the egg whites does; it adds lots of air into the mixture. When you put this in the oven, the heat causes air that has been trapped in bubbles in the egg white mixture to expand. The heat also causes the egg white to harden, making the solid structure of the soufflé.

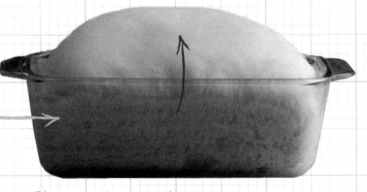

*Fig. 2* The bubbles of carbon cause the dough to rise

For soufflés, the all-important factor is less about chemistry and more about engineering. The structure of the soufflé needs to be strong enough to support its expanded volume. If it is too weak, tears appear in the structure or the air bubbles simply collapse in on themselves.

## Sound structures

To make sure your soufflé structure is strong enough, you need to keep your original mixture free from contamination. Egg white is largely composed of water and a mixture of proteins. Whisking separates these proteins and creates the foam.

One of the things that can undermine the strength of the structure is fat, which disrupts the egg white's ability to form a strong framework. Unfortunately, eggs have a readily available source of fat in the egg yolk. It is for this reason that to maintain your soufflé's proud rise, you need to avoid contaminating the egg white with any traces of egg yolk. Similarly, fatty or soapy deposits on a poorly cleaned mixing bowl can also weaken the foam structure.

So now you know the science, the next time you're in the mood for baking, you'll know how to avoid the disappointment of collapse and make sure your culinary efforts don't go to waste.

# How to improve your memory

We have all been there. You are introduced to someone at a party, and while talking with them you are called upon to use their name. Your mind is a blank despite having been told their name only moments before—your memory has failed you again.

It's not just names either. How often have you gone upstairs to fetch something, only to reach the top of the stairs and then stand there for minutes trying to recall exactly what you were doing? Or parked your car at the mall only to have trouble tracking it down when you return from shopping? There are things we can do to improve our memory.

## The science of our minds

Before looking at ways in which we can improve our memory, it is useful to look at how the brain and memory work from a scientific standpoint.

The human brain comprises billions of brain cells, known as neurons. Each neuron is interconnected to thousands of other neurons through what is known as a synapse. A chemical called a neurotransmitter passes signals between neurons across this synapse.

Brain scans using magnetic resonance imaging show that when you experience or learn something, various neurons in your brain become active. Recalling that experience or memory appears to require your brain to recreate that pattern of activation. However, the process is still not clearly understood.

Cognitive psychology, the study of how we store information in our brains, defines three different types of memory: sensory, short-term, and long-term. Sensory memory holds information on external stimuli, such as smells and noises, on a very short-term basis, typically less than a couple of seconds.

Some of this information is discarded and some is moved to the short-term memory. This memory allows us to hold between four and nine pieces of information in our brains for a period of 10 to 15 seconds, although the number of pieces of information retained in the short-term memory depends on the type of information being memorized.

Some of the information in the short-term memory is then transferred to our long-term memory by the process of repetition—the key to improving your memory, as we will see. Long-term memory appears to have a virtually unlimited capacity and no time limit. It is important to note that the processes by which the transfer of information occurs are the subject of much controversy.

## Making the most of memory

So how do we use this knowledge to our benefit? There are a number of methods you can use to try to improve your memory.

Playing brain training games is unlikely to help. A 2010 study of 11,430 people who played the games over a six-week period found that while participants improved at the games themselves, none of the skills were transferable. Researchers found that general reasoning, memory, planning, and visuospatial abilities did not improve as a result of playing the games.

### Repetition

It is the repetition element that transfers information to our long-term memories. When you are given new information that you need to remember, like a person's name, repeat that information out loud or to yourself as much as you can.

If you are introduced to someone named Ella, say: "Hi Ella, it's nice to meet you... What role do you have in your organization, Ella? Did you have a good trip here today, Ella? Great to meet you, Ella." Obviously, you should leave Ella the opportunity to respond or you may not be seeing her again any time soon.

## Chunking

The number of pieces of information retained in the short-term memory can be extended by a technique known as chunking—putting information together in small groups. For example, it is easier to remember a telephone number in groups of digits rather than as a string of single digits.

## Visual associations

Humans are also good at remembering pictures more easily than words. The trick is to associate the name with a picture in your mind.

For example, if you meet someone named Bill, think of Bill's face but with an added toucan's bill. Another option is to think of an object that rhymes with a name. If you meet a prospective client named Kate, you could come up with the rhyming word *skate*. Imagine a picture of Kate on ice skates. That strange image of her doing a pirouette on skates will help you when you meet her again.

Or break the name down into parts with visual associations. Say you met Penny Collingwood, how would you remember her name? The trick is to bring it down into words that can be visualized. Pen—knee—calling—wood. Imagine the picture of a woman with a fountain pen with a sharp nib that has fallen into her knee. She is calling the doctor while looking out of the window at the woods. It might sound a bit crazy but it does actually work.

## Mnemonics

Another technique to remember information is to use mnemonics—poems, words, sounds, or movements that create easily remembered connections to help organize related information. This is based on the idea that the average person finds it much easier to remember an actual phrase or personal, meaningful information than to recall pieces of random information. The most popular mnemonic devices are words or phrases made up of the first letters of the information you are trying to commit to memory. For example, remembering the names of the planets in order of their distance from the sun is easy when you use the phrase My Very Easy Method: Just Set Up Nine Planets—Mercury, Venus, Earth, Mars, Jupiter, Saturn, Uranus, Neptune, Pluto. Another popular one to remember the order of the points on a compass is Never Eat Shredded Wheat (North, East, South, West).

## The power of a nap

Taking a nap can also help improve your memory. Researchers at the University of Haifa's Center for Brain and Behavior Research carried out a study in which they asked participants to remember a sequence of thumb and finger movements. Those that took a nap did better. Although the mechanism is not entirely clear, the researchers believe that the nap allowed participants to consolidate their memory of the task better and also made it less prone to interference from other distractions.

# How to wrap presents

It's late on Christmas Eve and you have to make a quick decision. You have two final presents to wrap, but there's only one piece of wrapping paper left. Do you have enough for both or will you have to make a last-minute trip to the store?

People have their own favorite methods of wrapping presents. Even something as seemingly straightforward as a box can be handled in different ways. Some people start by taping the edge of the paper to one of the edges of the box and then rolling the paper around. Others place the box in the middle of a sheet and bring the ends of the paper together over the top. But is there a correct mathematical way to wrap presents that uses the least amount of paper?

## The science bit

One mathematician has studied gift wrapping in depth in order to find out how to use the least paper. Research by Warwick Dumas of the Department of Applied Mathematics at the University of Leicester shows that the least amount of paper required to wrap a typical box with sides of length $a$, $b$, and $c$ is given by this formula (see Fig. 1):

$$A = 2 \times (a \times b + a \times c + b \times c + c^2)$$

*Fig. 1 The perfect gift wrapping formula*

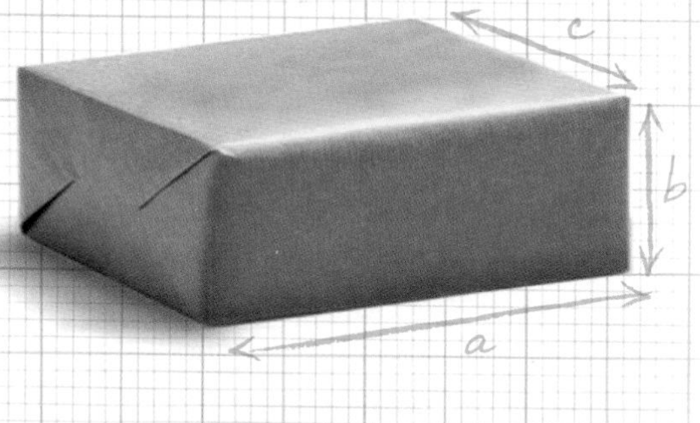

This equation comes from the areas of the six sides of the box added together plus a little bit extra (the $c^2$ bit) for a couple of flaps at either end.

## Wrapping your present

First make sure you have enough paper to wrap the box. There should be enough lengthwise to wrap around the box with, say, 2 inches to spare to create a neat overlap. So, if the box measures 5 inches by 10 inches on the two shortest sides, you need the paper to be at least 5 + 10 + 5 + 10 = 30 inches + 2 inches overlap = 32 inches long. Cut the wrapping paper to this length.

The width of the paper needs to be the width of the box plus half its height plus a little extra for the overlap. If our box is 15 inches wide, then we need 15 inches + 2½ inches (half its height) + 2 inches (overlap), or 19½ inches. Cut the paper to this width.

To make optimum use of the paper, start with the longest edge of the box you want to wrap parallel to the edge of the paper (see Fig. 2). Place the box a couple of centimeters in from the edge of the paper that is closest to you. Make sure the box is centrally placed so there are equal amounts of paper to the left and right. Keeping everything parallel, bring the far edge of the paper toward you and tuck it over the other edge. If you have measured correctly, there should be just enough to overlap by an inch or two. Pull the paper tight and stick the folded edge down onto the paper beneath.

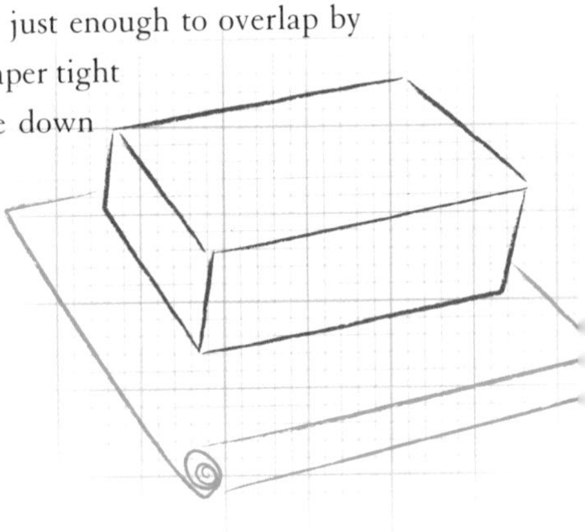

Fig. 2
Positioning the
box correctly

Next push the overhanging paper down at one end of the box to create two triangular flaps; be sure you don't push the present away from the center of the paper. Crease these two triangular flaps and then fold them to the center of the present. This action will create a triangle of paper at the bottom of the box. Crease the edges of this triangle and fold it up to the center, keeping the paper taut. Fix the flaps in place with a small piece of tape. Repeat this whole procedure at the other end. Your present is now wrapped.

## Diagonal wrapping

There are some people who like to wrap a present starting with it diagonal to the paper's edge (see Fig. 3). Mathematician Warwick Dumas has some bad news— doing this always uses at least as much paper (and usually more) as wrapping the present starting with it parallel to the edge.

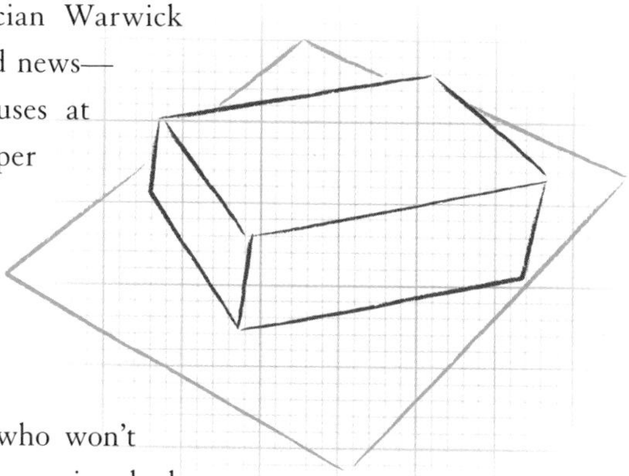

For those people who won't give up on diagonal wrapping, he has some further advice: if the depth of the present multiplied by two and a half is greater than the difference between the other two edges, then you should place the present at 45 degrees to use the least paper. Otherwise, he suggests tilting the present by the least amount possible so that when the flaps are folded over, they only just meet.

Fig. 3
Diagonally
wrapping a gift

## Oddly shaped presents

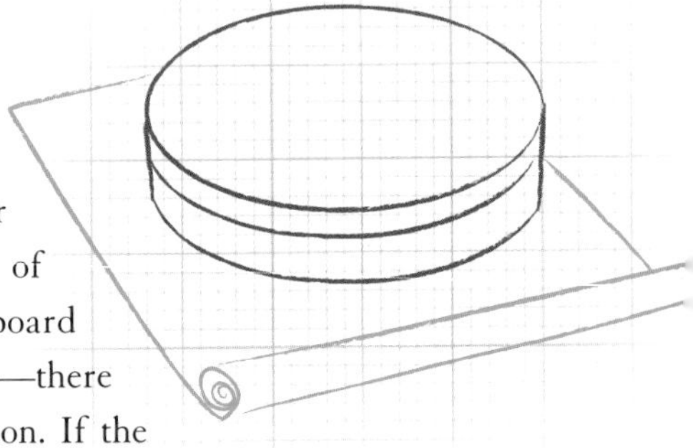

But what about odd shapes? Math can help here too. For cylinders—a bottle of whiskey in its cardboard container, for example—there are two courses of action. If the radius of the cylinder (the distance from the center of the circle on the top to the edge) is more than about

Fig. 4 Wrapping a circle

88 percent of the height, then you should wrap it as if it were a box shape (see Fig. 4). Otherwise, you should roll the wrapping paper around the cylinder with a few centimeters of overlap and the scrunch in the ends like rosettes (see Fig. 5).

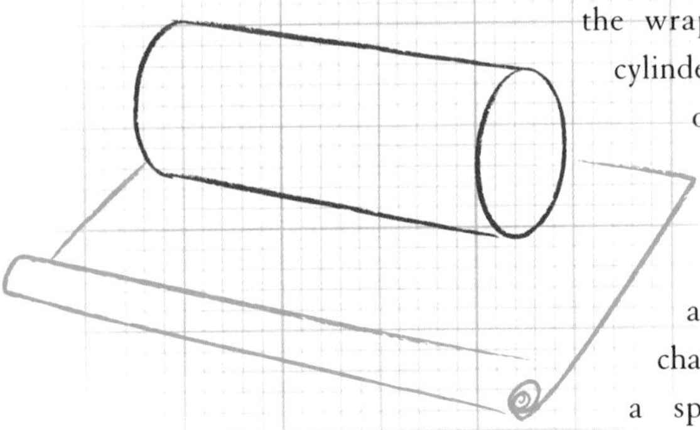

Spherical objects, such as balls, pose a particular challenge. The surface area of a sphere is given by the expression $2\pi d^2$ where $d$ is the diameter of the ball, so this is the minimum amount of paper you

Fig. 5 Wrapping a cylinder

would need. Achieving this in practice is difficult. You could get somewhere close by cutting your paper into petal shapes, although making it neat would be a challenge. Most people take the easy way out and put the ball in a box and wrap that.

# How to spin a ball

Watch a few games of baseball and you soon realize there are
many different ways to pitch a ball and that pitchers throw the
ball at different speeds in order to fool the batter. If all that
governed the flight of the ball were placement, speed, and
gravity, baseball—and many other sports such as basketball
or soccer—would be very boring to watch and require less
skill to play.

## The Magnus effect

Luckily, ball sports are not just a matter of throwing or kicking a
ball with the right amount of force in the desired direction.
Science shows us that if you throw a ball with spin, it curves
through the air, adding subtlety to many games. The science
behind spin lies with something called the Magnus effect.

The diagram below (Fig. 1) shows a spinning ball. The blue
arrowed lines represent the flow of air past the ball. The velocity
of the bottom part of the ball is in the same direction as the air

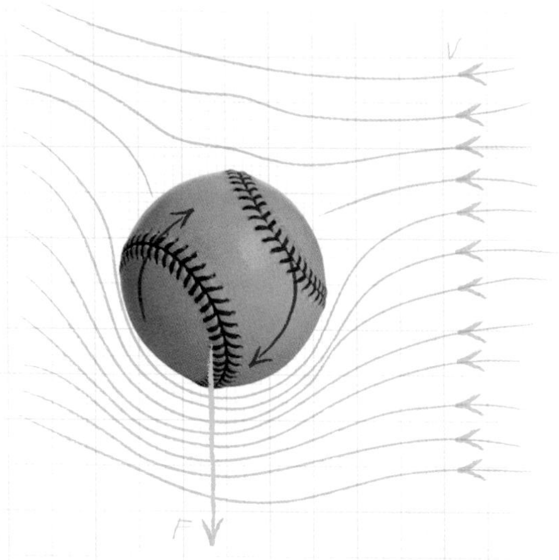

Fig. 1
The Magnus
effect

flow so gets added to it while the velocity of the top part of the ball is in the opposite direction and gets subtracted. The difference in velocity causes slight pressure differences in the air, resulting in a force in the direction of the blue arrow—the Magnus force that causes the bend.

The situation is complicated further because when a player initially hits or throws the ball, the air is not flowing smoothly around it. If the ball is thrown or hit hard enough, it will travel without spinning (and without bending) for a short distance and then start spinning and deviating from its original course.

## Up your game

So we can use our knowledge of the Magnus effect to improve our performance in sports—for example, to get a ball round the edge of a wall in soccer or to throw a curveball in baseball.

Spin makes a ball's trajectory much more unpredictable so pitchers can use the Magnus force to great effect. They can spin the ball in different directions and with different amounts of spin, depending on the action of the wrist and arm. The Magnus effect causes the ball to curve off its normal trajectory making it much more difficult to judge where it will go. The curveball, for example, where a pitch is given topspin, makes it drop faster than would normally happen under the influence of gravity.

The key to throwing a curveball is to get a grip on the ball's seam with your middle finger. When you release the ball, which should be close to the body, pull your hooked hand down in front of the body, using the wrist to impart spin to the ball, then let physics take its course.

The same idea can also apply to batting. In his 2007 paper "The Effect of Spin on the Flight of a Baseball," Alan M. Nathan at the University of Illinois shows just how the Magnus force can be

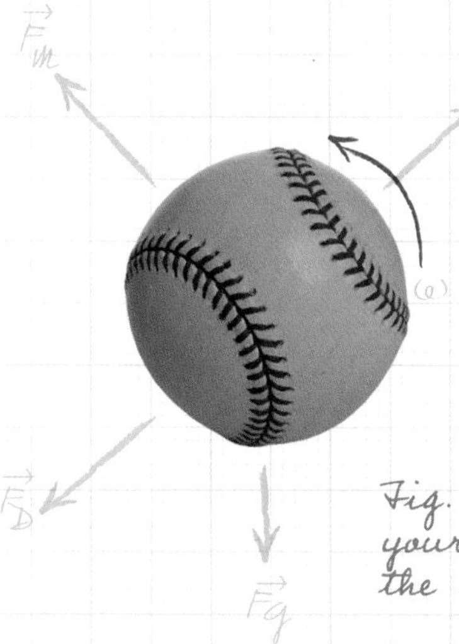

Fig. 2 Optimizing your spin using the forces of flight

used to increase your chances of hitting a home run. Nathan shows the forces acting on the baseball as above (see Fig. 2).

$F_D$ is the drag due to air, $v$ is the velocity, $F_G$ is the effect of gravity and $F_M$ is the Magnus force. $\omega$ is the angular velocity of the ball.

The paper shows how the size of the Magnus force is given by the following equation:

$$F_M = \tfrac{1}{2} C_L \rho A v^2$$

where $C_L$ is known as the lift coefficient, $\rho$ is the density of air, and $A$ is the cross-sectional area of the ball. In turn, $C_L$ is dependent on $\omega$, the angular velocity.

Since the angular velocity is a function of the amount of spin we put on the ball, we can work out that when you hit a baseball you should undercut it in order to give it more backspin. The backspin will increase the Magnus force, making it go higher in the air, and keeping it up in the air for longer. This is why you should undercut the baseball to give you a better chance of getting a home run.

# How to make your garden grow

Vegetable and fruit gardening can be a rewarding process. When you sit in the garden on a warm day and pick a fresh spear of asparagus or a crisp apple, all those hours spent on nurturing it during the cold and rainy periods suddenly seem worthwhile. Yet if you use the same patch year in year out to grow your fruits and vegetables, the soil can become starved of nutrients, making both the fruits and vegetables and the total crop smaller.

## Plant essentials

Plants use a system called photosynthesis to make the "food" they need to grow. In fact, it is the basis for all life on earth since the foods eaten by most animals, including humans, develop and grow in this way. The process of photosynthesis takes carbon dioxide and water and breaks it down using sunlight to create oxygen and carbohydrates, the latter being the food that sustains the plant.

So plants need three things to stay alive: carbon dioxide, water, and sunlight. Soil is also useful as it supports the structure of the plant, helps a plant gather water through the root system, and gives access to nutrients that help the plant grow faster. However, it is not essential. Virtually every plant can also be grown hydroponically—i.e., in water rather than soil. The plant takes any nutrients that have been dissolved in the water through its roots rather than from the soil.

## Process of photosynthesis

Photosynthesis uses carbon dioxide and water, releasing oxygen as a waste product. Your garden plants will get the carbon dioxide, water, and sunlight that they need for photosynthesis naturally outdoors (see Fig. 1). Since most of us grow our plants in soil rather than hydroponically, ensuring that you have the best soil and nutrients for your plants is where you can make a difference.

sunlight

$O_2$

Fig. 1 The process of photosynthesis

$CO_2$

$H_2O$

## Nutrients in soil

Often, particularly in vegetable gardens, the soil gets depleted of nutrients that help plants flourish. Many successful gardeners use compost to improve their soil. Composting sounds simple—you throw out your fruit and vegetable scraps, grass clippings, and other waste plant material, and months later it has miraculously turned into a rich, soil-like material that works wonders when mixed in with the topsoil in your garden.

In fact, there are ways of making sure that you have the best possible compost, by understanding the processes going on in your compost bin. After you throw in your leftover plant material, an army of animal life starts work. Worms, ants, mites, and beetles start munching their way through the material, breaking it down physically into smaller parts.

Then the microbes take over. Bacteria, fungi, and other small organisms start to oxidize the carbon compounds in the waste material. This is known as the mesophilic stage and usually lasts a few days. Their action on the waste produces heat, causing the temperature of the compost heap to rise.

After this initial period, thermophilic (heat-loving) organisms, particularly bacilli, take over and continue the breakdown of proteins and fat. This stage is also when the cellulose, the structural skeleton of plants, gets broken down into its constituent parts. As the supply of these materials dwindles, the temperature of the heap falls and the mesophilic organisms take over again. After a few months, and with a bit of luck, all that is left is a dark soil rich in basic nutrients, particularly nitrates.

# Even ratios

Making the best compost depends on getting conditions in the compost just right. In particular, the ratio of carbon to nitrogen is of prime importance. The bacteria and other microbes at the heart of the composting process work best with a C:N ratio of 30:1. Stray from this ratio and the rate of composting slows or the compost releases excess ammonia into the atmosphere. Dry, brown materials, such as sawdust, dry leaves, and straw, are generally high in carbon. Green leaves, such as vegetable waste from the kitchen, are generally high in nitrogen. Use this knowledge to try to keep close to the ideal ratio—i.e., put far more dry, brown material in than green.

# Moisture content

Having the right water content is also important. If the compost heap contains too much water, then it becomes sloppy and loses its structure. If you have too little moisture in the pile, the rate of composting decreases significantly. A moisture content of 55 to 70 percent is considered ideal, which looks like a wet sponge in practice. If it's too dry, just add some water.

The microbes that power composting need oxygen to thrive. While composting still works if there is little oxygen, the process is slower and your compost heap tends to be smellier. This is the reason why clever gardeners "turn" their compost—i.e., move the layers around to introduce oxygen into it. You should probably do this once a week.

# How soon do you need to apply your brakes?

Up ahead you see red tail lights flick on, and you instinctively press the brake pedal. If you have left enough distance between you and the car in front of you, then you will glide to a safe stop with plenty of space to spare. If not, you could end up with a severely dented fender, or much worse.

## Laws of motion

The physics of moving objects is known as mechanics. A number of equations of motion govern what happens to objects that are accelerating and decelerating. The ones of interest to us are as follows:

$$v = u + at$$

and

$$v^2 = u^2 + 2as$$

where $v$ is the final velocity, $u$ is the initial velocity, $a$ is the acceleration, $t$ is the amount of time over which the acceleration has occurred, and $s$ is the distance traveled.

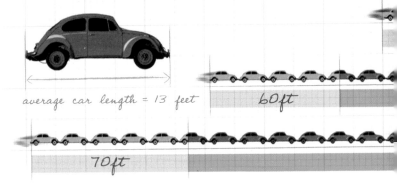

average car length = 13 feet

60ft

70ft

Everyone who has taken a driving test should be familiar with stopping distances in cars. Would-be drivers have to learn a table of typical distances that it takes for a car to stop at various speeds (see chart below). The stopping distance is the thinking and braking distances added together. Also included here is the speed in feet per second, to make the math easier for us.

What some people are surprised about is the rapid increase in the amount of distance it takes to stop, which goes up more quickly than the speed. For example, the stopping distance at a speed of 40 mph is more than double that at 20 mph.

| | mph | feet/s |
|---|---|---|
| *thinking distance* / *braking distance* | 20 | 29.3 |
| 20ft 20ft | Total = | 40ft |
| | 30 | 44 |
| 30ft 45ft | Total = | 75ft |
| | 40 | 56.6 |
| 40ft 80ft | Total = | 120ft |
| | 50 | 73.3 |
| 125ft | Total = | 175ft |
| | 60 | 88 |
| 180ft | Total = | 240ft |
| | 70 | 102.6 |
| 45ft | Total = | 315ft |

What the table now tells us is that experts believe that it takes us two-thirds of a second to react to brake lights showing up in front of us. You can see this by dividing any number in the thinking distance column by the corresponding figure in the car speed (in feet per second) column.

## How quickly can you stop?

So using the equations above, we can work out how quickly we brake (or decelerate), and how long it will take us to stop.

At 20 mph (or 29.3 ft/s), the braking distance is 20 feet. Let's plug this into our second equation, i.e. set $v = 0$, $u = 29.3$ ft/s and $s = 20$ feet, to work out how quickly we brake.

We can rearrange $v^2 = u^2 + 2as$ to give:

$$a = \frac{(v^2 - u^2)}{2s}$$

$$a = \frac{(0 - 858.49)}{2 \times 20}$$

or $a = -21.65$ feet per second.

(Note that the minus sign indicates that we are braking [decelerating] rather than accelerating.)

We can then use $v = u + at$ to work out how long it is going to take us to stop. Rearranging this gives:

$$t = \frac{(v - u)}{a}$$

$$t = \frac{(0 - 29.3)}{-21.65}$$

Or $t = 1.35$ seconds

Added to the thinking time it means it is going to take two seconds for us to stop.

# Bear in mind when driving...

These equations of motion are designed for situations involving constant acceleration or deceleration (braking). In real terms that means holding your foot at a constant position on the brake pedal in your car. However, science tells us that by increasing the deceleration (i.e., by pressing your foot down on the brake pedal), you will stop in a shorter distance than that listed in the chart.

The equations tell us how to work out the stopping distance and time for any speed, not just those in the chart. If you are planning to drive on Germany's autobahns, with no speed limits, you can use the equations to work out how much distance you should leave between the car in front and you.

From all of this, you can see how important the driver reaction time is. Improving your reaction time can help you stop in a much shorter distance. Halving your reaction time could save you 35 feet of thinking distance—that's more than two car lengths. In an accident, that could be just enough to make a difference.

# How to make the perfect cup of tea

Millions of cups of tea are consumed around the world every day, so it comes as no surprise that there is some debate over what constitutes the perfect way to make one. Should it have milk? Should the milk go in first or last? Should you warm the pot? Do you need to drink the tea from porcelain cups? Luckily, science has something to say about the subject.

As long ago as 1980, the International Organization for Standardization (ISO), which produces international standards on everything from the size of screw threads and steel wire to computer technology and environmental management, has had its own views on how to make a cup of tea. The standard goes by the grandiose name of "Tea—Preparation of Liquor for Use in Sensory Tests." The ISO does not claim that its method of making tea is perfect, but it does make the jobs of those who are paid to taste tea a lot easier, because it allows them to make valid comparisons.

* The teapot should be made from porcelain or earthenware and should weigh 4 oz (118 g) if it is small or 7 oz (200 g) if it is large, give or take a few grams.
* The pot should be filled to within 4 to 6 mm of its lid with freshly boiled water.
* The tea should be brewed for six minutes.
* If milk is required, this should be added first to avoid scalding it with the hot tea "liquor." The ISO says that the addition of milk is not essential, but it sometimes helps to accentuate differences in flavor and color.

Chemists have been drawn into the controversy over how to make a great cuppa. In 2003, the Royal Society of Chemistry (RSC) released its own formula.

## Use fresh water

They recommend filling the kettle with fresh, soft water. Dr. Andrew Stapley of Loughborough University adds, "Previously boiled water will have lost some of its dissolved oxygen which is important to bring out the tea flavor." If you use hard water to make tea, you will probably end up with tea scum floating on the top, thanks to the minerals dissolved in it.

## The perfect pot

The RSC then recommends warming the pot, which should be ceramic to avoid tainting the flavor of the tea, in the microwave first, ensuring it contains a small amount of water. You should then synchronize pouring away this water with the boiling of the kettle.

## Brewing time

Add one rounded teaspoon of leaves per person, and then pour the boiling water onto them, leaving them to brew for three minutes. The length of brewing is critical, says the society. "It is a myth that brewing for longer times causes more caffeine to infuse into the tea. Caffeine is a relatively

*brew for 3 minutes*

quick infuser and caffeine infusion is largely complete within the first minute. More time is, however, needed for the polyphenolic compounds (tannins) to come out which give the tea is color and some of its flavor. Infusing for longer times than this, however, introduces high molecular weight tannins which leave a bad aftertaste."

## On adding milk

The RSC says milk should be put into the cup first, followed by the tea, in order "to achieve a color that is rich and attractive," but also to stop denaturation of the milk, which impairs its taste. If milk is poured into hot tea, individual drops separate from the bulk of the milk and come into contact with the high temperatures of the tea for enough time for significant denaturation to occur. This is much less likely to happen if hot water is added to the milk."

In a non-scientific note, the RSC says that the tea should be enjoyed between 140° and 149°F (60° and 65°C) "to avoid vulgar slurping which results from trying to drink tea at too high a temperature."

# How to take the perfect photograph

The rise of the digital camera, where you can take thousands of shots and discard all but the best, has made us less discerning when it comes to composition of our photos than we might have been when we were limited to a roll of film you had to pay to process before you could see the results. Even so, perhaps sometimes you wish your vacation photos had a bit more of a professional or artistic air to them to do their subjects justice.

To get photos that will draw admiring comments, and to avoid wading through thousands of dreadful shots, you can apply some scientific methods to the business of framing your photo.

## The Golden Ratio

The study of something called the Golden Ratio stretches back more than 2,000 years, to the time of the Ancient Greeks. Pythagoras (of triangle theorem fame) was one of the first to consider the concept in great detail. (Greek mathematicians were interested in the ratio because of its use in geometry.)

In 1509, the Italian mathematician Luca Pacioli, a contemporary of Leonardo da Vinci, published a book called *De Divina Proportione*. The book covered how proportions were used not only in math but also in art and architecture. Following the publication, many Renaissance painters and architects used the Golden Ratio in their works, including da Vinci, believing it to be aesthetically pleasing.

Imagine you have a straight line divided into two parts, one of length $a$ and one of length $b$ as shown on the following page. The total length of the line is therefore $a + b$.

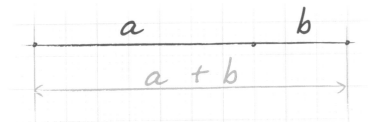

The Golden Ratio, usually denoted by the Greek letter phi ($\Phi$), is then where the following applies:

$$\phi = \frac{a + b}{a} = \frac{a}{b}$$

and is equal to 1.618033... (the digits after the decimal point continue forever; it is what is known as an irrational number).

## Fibonacci sequence

Why should the Golden Ratio have any effect on art? One answer might be found in something called Fibonacci numbers. This is a sequence of numbers as follows:

$$1 \quad 1 \quad 2 \quad 3 \quad 5 \quad 8 \quad 13 \quad 21 \quad 34 \quad 55 \quad 89 \quad ...$$

Each number in the sequence (which continues on forever) is equal to the previous two numbers added together, e.g., 89 = 34 + 55. What is interesting is what happens if you divide each number by the previous number. What you find is that the answer to this division fluctuates about a fixed number, getting closer and closer to that value as you move along the sequence. For example, 89 divided by 55 equals 1.61818... Look familiar? In fact as you move along, the ratio of consecutive numbers gets closer and closer to the Golden Ratio.

## Numbers in nature

So the Golden Ratio is hugely important in the Fibonacci series, but the Fibonacci series is also important in nature. The number of shoots and petals as well as the patterns of seeds in seedheads of flowers often follows a Fibonacci sequence.

The swirling spiral of a nautilus shell also appears constructed according to the sequence (see Fig. 1). We can construct a spiral by drawing adjacent squares with side lengths of the numbers in the Fibonacci sequence. In each of these squares, we then draw a quarter circle. The resulting spiral looks remarkably similar to the nautilus, and its construction is inextricably linked to the Golden Ratio.

It is perhaps this link with nature that was so appealing to Renaissance artists, encouraging them to believe that by using the Golden Ratio in their works, they were following in the footsteps of God (or Mother Nature at the very least).

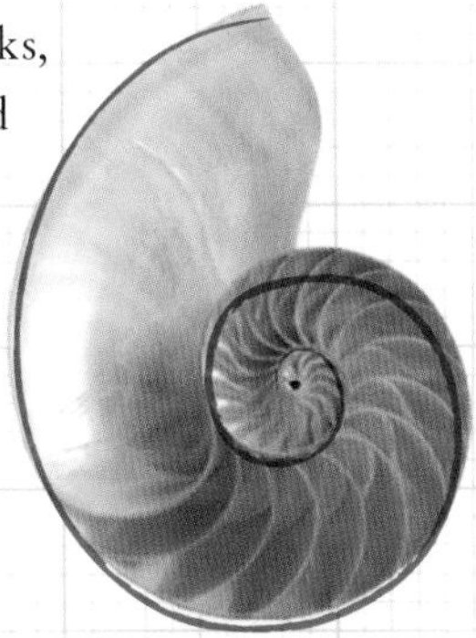

*Fig. 1 A mathematical representation of the Fibonacci sequence*

89

1

8

5

1

0

2

13

55

3

21

34

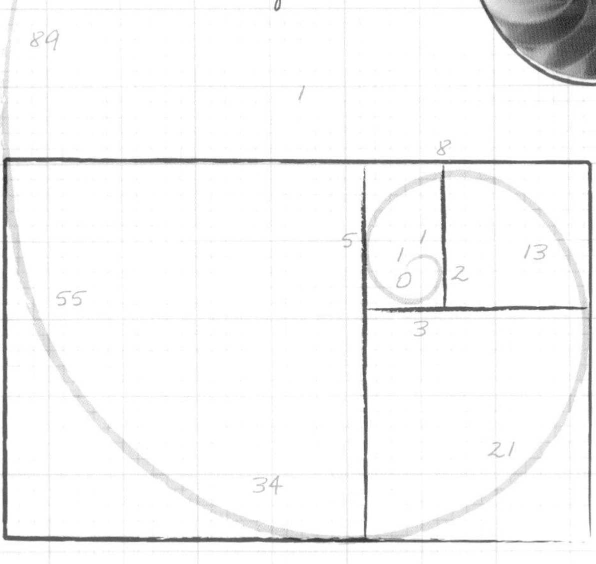

## Golden Ratio in photography

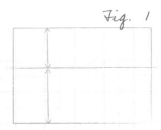

Fig. 1

To use the Golden Ratio in creative work, consider the rectangular viewfinder of your camera. We can draw an imaginary straight line dividing the viewfinder up into the proportions specified by the Golden Ratio (Fig. 1).

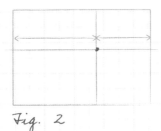

Fig. 2

We can do the same with a vertical line, too, and see where the two lines cross, at the point marked in red (Fig. 2). By considering symmetry, we can see there are three other similar points on the viewfinder (Fig. 3).

Now the interesting part is to use those imaginary red dots. When you are lining up a shot, rather than placing the most important part of the subject of your photo right in the center of the picture, place it at one of these points.

Fig. 3

For example, if you are taking a picture of a face, put the eyes or the smile at one of these points. If you are taking a picture of a

landscape, try to find a point of interest in the scene, such as a lonely sheep on a hillside or a duck bobbing on the water, and place it at the point.

Take a look at these three pictures. In the first photo, the

desert island is centered, and you might say that it is an attractive scene. However, if we move the camera to place the island at one of our imaginary red dots, we get the third photo. Most people feel subconsciously that in this picture the composition is better, although most are not sure why—they just have a gut feeling.

Another technique is to lead the eye of anyone looking at the photo from the corner of the photo to these red points by using some element of the scene, a path, a walkway, the line of a fence, for example, while yet another composition technique uses the spiral constructed by Fibonacci numbers as a way of guiding viewers' eyes to one of the red points. So, as we've seen, math even has a part to play in art.

# How to throw a ball farther

Throwing a ball is one of the first things we learn as a youngster, but it can be difficult to do well. Why is it that only a few of us turn into world-class baseball pitchers while the rest of us have difficulty getting the ball more than a few feet away from where we threw it? What these world-class sportsmen and women know instinctively is the science behind throwing a ball. The science combines diverse elements such as gravity, ballistics, and human physiology.

## Following the trajectory

What determines the path or trajectory of a ball after it leaves your hand? If you are unsure, you are not alone. It took scientists centuries of studying the paths of objects—particularly cannon and musket balls—to work out what was going on.

It was the Italian mathematician and scientist Galileo Galilei who first realized the importance of gravity

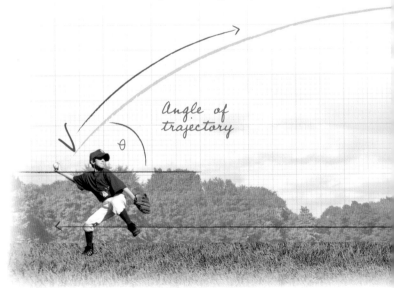

Angle of trajectory

θ

in the trajectory of an object. After the ball leaves your hand, gravity pulls the ball down to the ground.

First, we need to consider the velocity at which you release the ball, which we call $v$. Since velocity is a vector (as it has a direction), you can break it down into vertical and horizontal components, $v_v$ and $v_h$, which will obey the following:

$$v_v = v \sin\theta$$

$$v_h = v \cos\theta$$

where $\theta$ is the angle between the path of the ball and the ground as shown (see Fig. 1).

If there is no drag due to air, then $v_h$ remains constant throughout the trajectory. However, $v_v$ does not. If you take a snapshot of the ball at the highest point of the trajectory, then you can see that it is stationary in the vertical direction—i.e., at that point $v_v$ is zero.object.

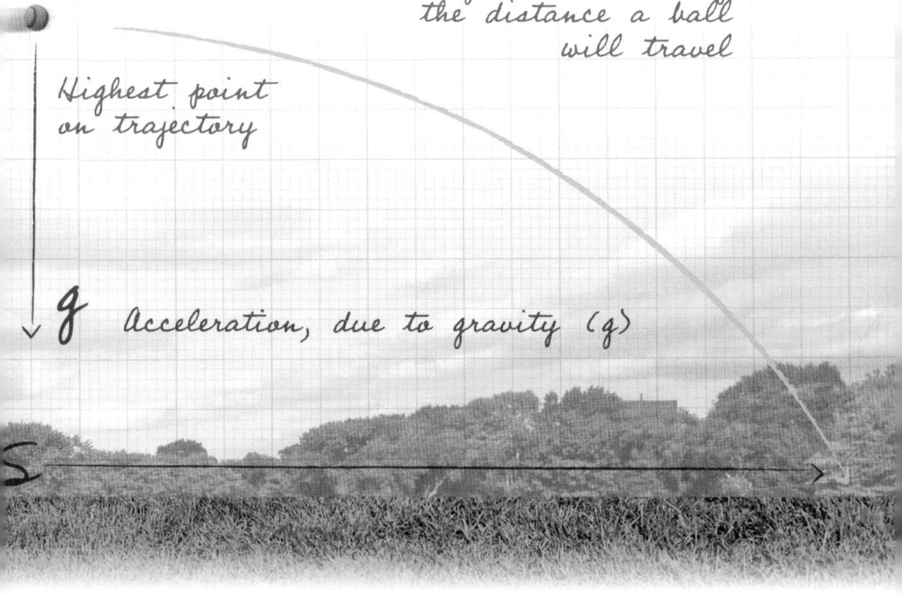

Fig. 1 Calculating the distance a ball will travel

Highest point on trajectory

$g$ Acceleration, due to gravity (g)

We can use an equation of motion to find out how long it takes to reach this highest point:

$$v = u + at$$

where $v$ is the final velocity, $u$ is the initial velocity, $a$ is the acceleration, and $t$ is the time. Looking at just the vertical component of velocity and considering the journey from release to the highest point we get:

$$0 = v_v - gt$$

Since the "final" velocity is zero at the top, $v_v$ is the initial vertical component of the velocity and $t$ is the time taken to reach that top point. Notice that we have set $a = -g$ where $g$ is the acceleration due to gravity (9.8 meters per second squared). The minus sign indicates that it is a deceleration rather than an acceleration.

Therefore the time to reach the top of the trajectory is:

$$t = \frac{v_v}{g} = \frac{v \sin\theta}{g}$$

Since this is the time for reaching the top, the total journey time of the ball, which we shall call $T$, is twice this or:

$$\frac{2v \sin\theta}{g}$$

Since the horizontal velocity is constant, we know that the distance traveled by the ball ($s$) is the horizontal velocity multiplied by this total time:

$$s = v_h \times T$$

or

$$s = \frac{v \cos\theta \times 2v \sin\theta}{g} = \frac{2v^2 \sin\theta \cos\theta}{g}$$

Since $g$ is a constant, this shows that the distance the ball travels depends on the initial velocity and, crucially, the angle at which you throw the ball.

## Judging the angle

As the velocity will be limited by your own physical strength, the angle is clearly an important consideration. We can take this mathematical discussion further. By using a process known as differentiation, we can work out which angle is the best to throw at. (We won't do it here but for anyone who wants a challenge, you need to work out the differential $ds/d\,\theta$ and set it to zero.) Using this differentiation, you can calculate that the best angle to throw the ball is at 45 degrees to the horizontal.

However, there are other factors to consider in the real world—drag and wind. Drag from the air rapidly decelerates the ball (the force due to drag is proportional to the square of the velocity) while a gust of wind can blow a ball off its trajectory.

You also need to consider the interplay between velocity and angle. The calculations assume that you are able to throw at a fixed velocity at whatever angle you choose to throw, but the mechanical restrictions of muscles in the body means that is not the case.

In 2006, Nicholas Linthorne and David Everett at the School of Sport and Education at Brunel University used video analysis to show that the best angle for a soccer throw-in is around 30 degrees from the horizontal, since they are able to throw it faster than at an angle of 45 degrees. The research also indicated that the best angle differs slightly from 30 degrees from player to player depending on their body size, muscular strength, and throwing technique.

# How to sail a yacht

To be a good sailor you need to understand both physics and math. Some people imagine that yachts work just by the wind filling the sail from behind and pushing it forward. That is certainly true if you are going in exactly the same direction as the wind, but common sense also tells us that sailing directly into the oncoming wind is a bad idea—you make no headway in the same way that walking against a strong wind is virtually impossible.

## Sailing forces

If you have ever watched a race, you will realize that yachts do not only ever travel in the direction of the wind—it would make for a rather uninteresting spectator sport not to mention an impractical means of transportation. They can travel in virtually any direction other than directly into the wind.

What enables this travel is lift—the same force that keeps airplanes in the air. The sail acts a little like a plane's wing, shaped so that wind travels over one side faster than the other, reducing the air pressure on that side. This difference in pressure between the two sides generates the lift pushing the sail in a direction perpendicular to the sail itself.

This lift can be very strong and would tend to push the yacht sideways rather than forward. However, there is another type of lift acting on the boat. Yachts have keels that dip into the water and these generate lift as water flows past them, but it acts in the opposite direction to the aerodynamic lift produced by the sail, cancelling out this sideways motion but leaving a component of the force in the forward direction.

Modern yachts can travel anywhere between 35 degrees and 90 degrees from the direction of the wind, depending on the design of the yacht. The smaller number refers to racing yachts, such as those in the America's Cup and Olympics.

In order to travel in the direction of the wind, you therefore need to sail in a zig-zag path, a process called beating. At the end of each leg, the boat needs to change tack—i.e., change the direction of the bow from one side to the other.

The momentum of the yacht carries it through the point where the boat is sailing directly into the wind. Clearly this means that you travel farther than you would to sail directly where you want. Unfortunately, it is the only option available.

## Full speed ahead

How can you make the yacht sail faster and win a race? It may seem counterintuitive, but traveling with the apparent wind almost perpendicular to the boat—called reaching—is the fastest way to travel, although the effect of wave crests in the water hitting the bow may actually make it less than optimum. So the important thing is to consider the apparent wind rather than the real wind. The apparent wind is the combined effect of the headwind (the wind opposed to the course of a moving object, in this case, the boat) and the real wind.

Since these can have different directions and sizes, you need to add them as vectors. The diagram on the following page (Fig. 1) shows the velocity of the yacht ($V$), the headwind ($H$), the wind ($W$), and the apparent wind ($A$). It is this apparent wind that acts on the sail to generate aerodynamic lift, and the greater it is, the faster you can go.

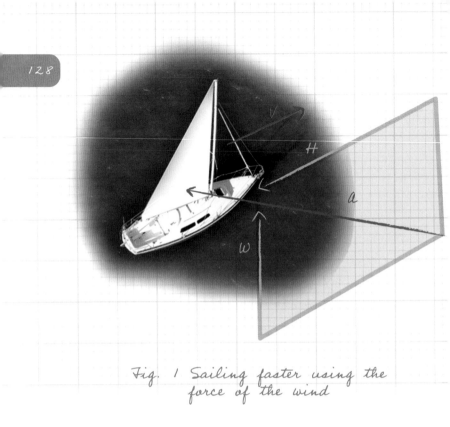

*Fig. 1 Sailing faster using the force of the wind*

### Beating the course

Competitive yacht races are often sailed on a triangular course. The Olympic triangle is an equilateral triangle, with each side the same length and 60 degree angles between each leg.

However, some races use a modified triangle with unequal sides, and sailors will then be required to resort to a little trigonometry and the sine rule in particular.

If you know the length of the windward leg in the race and can measure or make assumptions about the angles, you can calculate how long the other legs are, allowing you to work out the best tactics for getting around the course.

# How to swim faster

Humans are not natural swimmers, unlike some other mammals, and have to learn how to do it well. Most of us are recreational swimmers—we won't be winning any gold medals any time soon. But if you want to improve your time a little (or if you need to get out of the water in a hurry!), there are ways in which you can change your technique to learn how to swim faster and more efficiently.

## Negative forces

The speed and direction of a moving object are affected by the various forces acting upon it, and it is no different for a swimmer. Pulling you down is gravity while keeping you afloat is buoyancy. Pushing you forward are the forces generated by your legs and your arms while holding you back is drag, the resistive force of the water on your body. Gravity we can do little about, but examining how we can reduce drag can help us swim faster.

Clearly, going forward faster and with more power is vital. Two of the most important factors in swimming fast are stroke frequency and stroke length. The best performance is achieved by a combination of the two. Churning your arms as fast as you can, for example, is likely to not only wear you out much more quickly, but also reduce your stroke length. At the same time, however, physics tells us that the drag increases rapidly as your speed increases, so clearly, minimizing drag is the key.

We can do this through a combination of improved techniques (moving your arms, torso and legs in the most effective way, which you can clearly see in the difference in speed between various types of stroke: the front crawl is faster than breaststroke, for example) and by streamlining your body as much as you can to present the least possible resistance as you move through the water. Streamlining your body is without doubt the most useful way to improve your swimming for the same reason that car and aircraft designers try to reduce the drag on their fastest racing cars and planes.

## Reducing drag

One way to reduce your drag through the water is to be aware of your center of weight, usually in the chest for most people. By pushing your chest forward into the water with each stroke, this causes your hips to rise, making sure you don't sink too far into the pool, which increases the drag as you swim.

## Streamlining

Try to keep your body streamlined as you make a stroke. Take breaststroke, for example. The portion of the stroke that gives you the most forward propulsion is when you kick your legs like a frog. Your arms give you some propulsion but nowhere near as much. You should try to streamline your body most of all when making this most propulsive movement (see Fig. 1). As a result, when you pull your arms back, they should continue accelerating back through to the front, ensuring they are pointing straight ahead when you kick.

The position of your head can also be streamlined to increase your speed. Many swimmers look straight ahead when they breathe during the breaststroke, but this greatly increases drag. You should keep your head looking down in the water until you need to breathe. Raise your head just enough to take a breath but keep your chin tucked down onto your chest.

Drag is greatly reduced in front crawl because your arm returns to the front through the air rather than the water. You can further streamline your body though by keeping your arm close to your body, and by making sure your hand enters the water with the thumb or middle finger first to reduce turbulence.

## Getting a head start

It is hard to underestimate the value of achieving a good start. Whether you are diving in from a starting block or just pushing off from a wall, the advice is the same. The gravity assist of the dive and the spring effect of pushing off the wall mean you will initially move through the water faster than you can swim. To get the maximum benefit from this, you need to slide through the water as smoothly as you can, which again means streamlining your body. The most effective position is the one you see Olympic swimmers use all the time—they tuck their head into their collarbones, their biceps by their ears, passing their arms over their tucked-in head, and pointing them out straight ahead. You

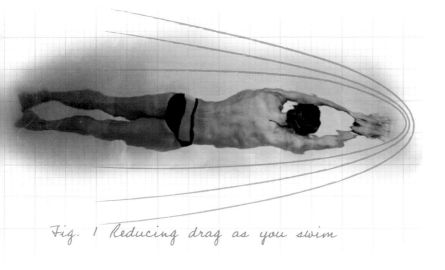

Fig. 1 Reducing drag as you swim

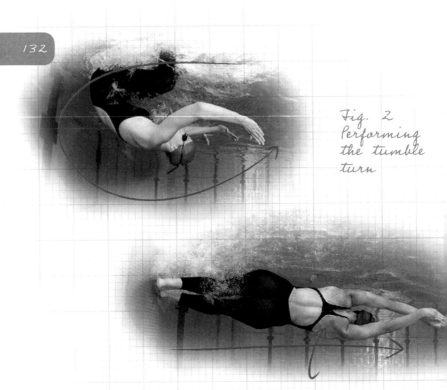

*Fig. 2*
*Performing*
*the tumble*
*turn*

should also aim to travel under the water for as long as possible in this position since breaking the water's surface increases drag.

One additional tip to increase your speed: learn how to use the wall of the swimming pool when turning. If you swim up to it, come to a stop, turn around and then start swimming again, you have lost valuable time and also disrupted your rhythm. Learning how to do a tumble turn when you approach the end of the pool will make your overall swimming time much faster. The turn begins with a somersault, followed by a push-off from the side of the pool, while rotating the body, keeping the arms extended above the head to streamline the upper body (see Fig. 2).

# Super suits

Science has also been used to reduce drag in another, more controversial, way. After the Beijing Olympics, South African sport scientists Ross Tucker and Jonathan Dugas looked at the longevity of world records in swimming compared to athletics. The difference is astounding. It shows that the average women's swimming world record stands for just eight months before being broken.

They say: "Records are broken with an extraordinary regularity. Part of this is the sport—swimming does lend itself to more frequent records, because small changes in things like technique, body position, and training can produce relatively large effects on performance."

They add that the current spate of breaking world records has more to do with advances in swimsuit technology. In 2008, 108 swimming world records were broken. What is more interesting is that 79 of them were broken by swimmers wearing the same swimsuit—the Speedo LZR. The ultratight suit is welded rather than stitched, has special polyurethane panels designed by NASA, and was believed to create extra buoyancy by trapping air. The international swimming authority, FINA, finally agreed that something was amiss with the suit and other similar copycats and banned them in January 2010. From now on, men's swimsuits must not extend above the navel nor below the knee, and women's must not cover the neck. They must also be made from "textiles."

FINA's rules on swimsuits only apply to Olympic Games and World Championships. Some national swimming authorities have also adopted the ban but not at every level of the sport. If your swim meet is not covered by the new rules, space-age swimsuits like the Speedo LZR clearly give you the edge.

# How to lift heavy loads

The pyramids of Giza in Egypt and Stonehenge in England are wonders of the ancient world. Many people have wondered how the architects and builders of the day could have possibly built them given the enormous weight of the stones that went into their construction. What is certain is that they used mechanics to give them an advantage and it is something that you can use, too, to help you lift heavier weights than you would normally manage.

## Levers and fulcrums

To see how we can lift heavy loads safely, we need to look at the world of mechanics and levers in particular. In mechanics, a lever is an object, such as a metal bar, that can be used to multiply the force applied to an object.

It is useful to define a few terms using the picture below:

effort   lever   fulcrum   load

The Greek mathematician Archimedes knew all about the advantage that a lever could give you. He was quoted as saying "Give me a place to stand, and I shall move the earth." By this he meant that with a long enough lever and an appropriately placed fulcrum, a person could lift the massive weight of the earth.

The physical quantity that is relevant here is *the moment of force,* which represents the tendency of a force to cause rotation. In our diagram, a load placed on the right of the lever causes it to rotate about the fulcrum, causing effort on the left-hand side.

In a simple situation like that in the diagram, the moment of force $M$ is given by the force applied multiplied by the distance to the fulcrum ($M = Fd$).

## Balancing seesaws

When a lever system is in equilibrium, all of these moments of force balance. Imagine the case of two children of equal weight sitting at equal distances from the center at either end of a seesaw. If they sit there without pushing off the ground with their legs, they remain in equilibrium—i.e., the seesaw does not move.

Now one child gets off and is replaced by a parent. Physics tells us that the seesaw now goes down at the parent's end, which is now the heavier end. However, if the parent moves closer to the center of the seesaw, this restores the former equilibrium (see Fig. 2).

We can see this at work in the moment of force equation. In a situation of equilibrium we can say that the moments of force of the child and adult are equal, i.e.:

$$M_{child} = F_{child} \times d_{child} = M_{adult} = F_{adult} \times d_{adult}$$

where $d$ is the distance from the center of the seesaw to where they are sitting.

We can measure the distance fairly easily but how about the force? Newton's law of motion comes in here. Newton tells us that $F = ma$ where $m$ is the mass of an object and $a$ is the acceleration of the object. On the seesaw, the only acceleration acting on the child and adult is the acceleration due to gravity, which we represent with the letter $g$. This means we can rewrite our equation as

$$m_{child} \times g \times d_{child} = m_{adult} \times g \times d_{adult}$$

Since $g$ is a constant and not zero we can divide it out of the equation to give

$$m_{child} \times d_{child} = m_{adult} \times d_{adult}$$

or

$$d_{adult} = \frac{m_{child} \times d_{child}}{m_{adult}}$$

So we can use this equation to work out how close the adult needs to sit to the center of the seesaw to balance the child.

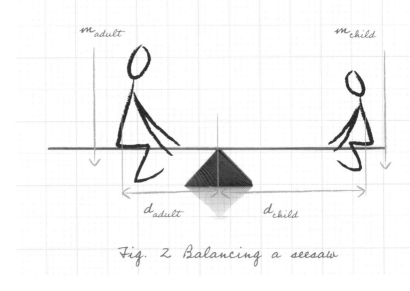

Fig. 2 Balancing a seesaw

Fig. 3 Using a lever to lift a heavy weight

## Using levers to lift weights

We use moments of force in our everyday life in many ways. A wheelbarrow, for example, allows us to lift a weight that would normally be too heavy for us, by applying an upward force at a long distance from the wheel, which acts as the fulcrum, to lift a weight which sits at a shorter distance to the fulcrum (see Fig. 3). We can use a similar formula to before:

$$m_{assisted} \times d_{tray} = m_{unassisted} \times d_{handles}$$

or

$$m_{assisted} = \frac{m_{unassisted} \times d_{handles}}{d_{tray}}$$

where $m_{assisted}$ is the amount you can lift in a wheelbarrow, $m_{unassisted}$ is the amount you can lift unassisted, $d_{handles}$ is the distance from the wheel to the handles, and $d_{tray}$ is the distance from the wheel to the center of the tray which holds the load. Since $d_{handles}$ is larger than $d_{tray}$, you can see that this setup gives you a mechanical advantage.

# How to avoid a hangover

Most of us have overdone it on a night out and had one drink too many at least a few times in our lives. It seems like a good idea at the time, but when you wake up the next morning, the mother of all hangovers is there with you in bed. How could it have all gone so wrong?

## Behind the pain

What, exactly, is a hangover? It is not just one thing, but a collection of symptoms, ranging from tiredness and thirst to headaches and vomiting. This variety of symptoms is caused by a combination of factors including, but not limited to, dehydration, imbalance of electrolytes in the body, sleep disruption, low blood sugar, and the contributory effects of other drugs, especially nicotine.

The dehydration occurs because alcohol is a diuretic—it makes you expel more liquid as urine than you consume in your alcoholic drinks.

## Acetaldehyde

The buildup of acetaldehyde in the system is also blamed for hangovers. Alcohol (ethanol) is broken down in the liver by an enzyme called alcohol dehydrogenase, which converts it to acetaldehyde, which has both toxic and carcinogenic (cancer-causing) properties in the human body. The enzyme acetaldehyde dehydrogenase then breaks this down to relatively harmless acetic acid (the acid in vinegar). Women have lower levels of alcohol dehydrogenase, which is one of the reasons that they tend to suffer worse hangovers than men, as scientific studies have shown. Biologically women tend to weigh less, have a higher percentage of body fat, and a lower percentage of total body water than most men, and so the alcohol is less diluted when it reaches their organs. Combined with their lower levels of alcohol dehydrogenase, alcohol tends to have a greater effect on women, both in levels of intoxication at the time, and in the effects of the subsequent hangover.

## Lucky genes

Interestingly, some people of Asian descent have mutations in their alcohol and acetaldehyde dehydrogenase genes which cause acetaldehyde to build up far more rapidly than normal, leading to rapid and severe hangovers. Other people never experience a hangover at all. A 2008 study by Jonathan Howland et al. of the Youth Alcohol Prevention Center at Boston University School of Public Health, which examined earlier studies as well as carrying out its own trials, found that an average of 23.6 percent of people never experienced a hangover.

The survey also found no evidence to support one anecdotal finding about hangovers: that drinks containing high levels of congeners, such as red wine, whiskey, and brandy, give you worse hangovers. Congeners are the other biological compounds in a drink that alter its appearance, taste, and smell.

Since a hangover is a combination of symptoms with a number of causes (some of which are poorly understood), curing one is a challenge. However, a combination of techniques can be applied.

## Rehydration

It might seem obvious, but since alcohol dehydrates you, drinking water while you drink alcohol, before you go to bed, and in the morning is essential. You need to make up for the liquid lost through urination. Dehydration is the most common symptom of a hangover, but it is also generally the cause of most of the other unpleasant effects.

## Eat, drink, be merry

"Lining your stomach" by drinking milk or eating food before you go out is often touted as a means of hangover prevention or reduction. This is because alcohol is absorbed through the lining of the stomach, and having something in your stomach before you start drinking slows the process down. The alcohol still reaches your bloodstream but over a longer period. However, research shows that the effect is relatively small.

## Hair of the dog

There is also some evidence that hangovers are in part caused by alcohol withdrawal. The severity of a hangover is, as you might expect, loosely connected to the amount of alcohol you consume and the duration of drinking. The peak level of a measure known as blood alcohol concentration (BAC), which is a percentage of the ratio of volume of alcohol to volume of blood in the body, is a particularly useful measure. At levels below 0.1%, the effects of drinking are generally positive—euphoria, talkativeness, and relaxation—however, as soon as you go over that level, the negative effects start to dominate. What is interesting is that the hangover often peaks when the BAC is passing through zero, indicating that at least some of the impact is brought about by alcohol withdrawal.

The view that hangovers are caused, at least in part, by alcohol withdrawal gives the basis for what people call "the hair of the dog (that bit you)," whose name derives from the idea that you could cure illnesses by using a part of whatever caused the illness in the first place (rather like homeopathy). However, scientists say that relief is at best temporary and at worst ineffectual and may lead to alcoholism.

## Reach for the medicine cabinet

One of the best remedies is a diarrhea remedy—rehydration salts—consumed before you go to bed. These can combat dehydration and low blood sugar as well as electrolyte imbalance. Drinking alcohol gives you a sugar rush and the body creates insulin to combat this. However, it can go too far and reduce blood sugar below normal levels. The rehydration salts raise the level of sugar and electrolytes in your system, as well as helping to rehydrate you.

Failing all else, you can reach for the painkillers. However, some, such as aspirin, can damage the stomach lining. Given that drinking alcohol does the same, you are risking damaging your stomach seriously, potentially leaving yourself prone to stomach ulcers.

Clearly the best way to avoid a hangover, other than to drink in moderation, is to keep up your fluid levels with plenty of water. Otherwise be prepared to pay for your evening out the next day!

# Index

## Picture credits

The publishers would like to thank the following for permission to reproduce pictures:

Dreamstime: pp. 14, 34, 44, 47, 58, 61, 64, 68, 71, 72, 75, 80, 82, 96, 103, 105, 110, 111, 113, 119, 122, 125, 138; iStockphoto: pp. 9, 13, 16, 21, 22, 25, 27, 30, 31, 34, 37, 39, 40, 41, 42, 49, 51, 62, 66, 72, 84, 85, 87, 89, 91, 92, 93, 94, 107, 115, 121, 122, 128, 131, 132, 134, 136, 137, 141.